Gordon Savage.

From
CARLISLE
and
OLD
CUMBERLAND

Laurie Kemp

BOOKCASE

*The grave of Robert Anderson, watercolour by Thomas Bushby.
Courtesy of Tullie House, Carlisle.*

Contents

George Moore: *The Merchant and Philanthropist from Wigton*	5
John Losh: *The Soldier from Wreay*	24
Jonathan Boucher: *Washington's Friend from Blencogo*	33
Duke of Norfolk: *The Convivial Aristocrat from Greystoke*	43
Thomas Bouch: *The Civil Engineer from Thursby*	49
Janet Woodrow: *The President's Mother from Carlisle*	54
Martin Tallents: *Carer for Robert Graves from Hutton End*	59
Henry Scott Sawyer: *The Malayan Adventurer from Carlisle*	67
William George Armstrong: *Mayor of Newcastle from Wreay*	71
John Robertson Scott: *The Countryman from Wigton*	75
Arthur C Astor: *The Man of the Theatre from Silloth*	83
Robert Anderson: *The Cumberland Bard from Carlisle*	88
John Heysham: *The Doctor from Carlisle*	154
Josiah Relph: *The Poet and Schoolmaster from Sebergham*	158
Joseph Simpson: *The Society Artist from Carlisle*	165
John Taylor and Robert Bowman	175
James Wallace: *The Attorney General from Brampton*	178

Copyright: Laurie Kemp, 2008.
ISBN 978-1-904147-34-3
First edition 2008
Published by Bookcase. Bookscumbria.com
19 Castle Street, Carlisle, CA3 8SY
01228 544560. bookcasecarlisle@aol.com.

Printed and bound by CPI Antony Rowe, Eastbourne

GEORGE MOORE

The Merchant and Philanthropist from Wigton

Fitful flickers from the oil-lamp light lit the scene as the yawning ostlers busied themselves leading the horses to be hitched up to the stage-coach which stood in the cobbled yard of Carlisle's Gray Goat Inn. It was a late winter's morning, shortly before 5a.m., the time when the London coach would clatter its way out under the arch and onto the road to begin its long journey south.

Keeping an eye on his luggage, a large hair trunk bequeathed to him by a great-uncle who was also his godfather, was a young man well-wrapped against the early morning chill. He was George Moore. He was leaving behind a boyhood spent on the family's Cumbrian farm and an apprenticeship to a draper in Wigton. He eventually found a career as one of London's leading merchants, became one of the city's leading charity workers, and the leader of a mission that supplied food to the starving citizens of a Paris after suffering a siege by a German army. Later, this Cumbrian farmer's son led the life of a country gentleman.

George had been born in 1806 at Mealsgate, the third son of a family of five. His father was a 'statesman' - a landholder - and the family had farmed at Overgate for more than three hundred years.

He began his schooling under an eccentric master at Boltongate. The school building stood at the corner of Bolton churchyard and was separated from the church by the parish burial ground. George later was to recall: "The master, Blackbird Wilson, was an old man, fond of drink. The scholars were sent out to fetch it for him three or four times a day. He used to drive the learning into us with a thick ruler, which he brought down sharply upon our backs. The wonder is that he did not break our skulls. Perhaps he calculated on their thickness. His rule was to drive reading, writing and arithmetic into

George Moore's birthplace in Mealsgate.

us by brute force. He never attempted to make learning attractive."

The eccentric schoolmaster had earned the nick-name 'Blackbird' by his uncanny ability to imitate the singing of any bird, but especially the blackbird.

The school had its daily routine. Another old pupil, the Reverend William Gunson, remembered that: "The fire was lighted in the mornings and the school swept out by two of the boys in turn, specially told off for the purpose. Their duty lasted for a week, at the end of which they had the privilege of naming their succesors for the following week. When coals were wanted, the money to buy them was raised by levying a tax of twopence or three half-pence on all the scholars."

After Boltongate George was sent to Pedlar Thommy's school at Crookdake, near Leegate. Schoolmaster Thommy had indeed once been a pedlar, and not a succesful one, but now was seen fit enough to run a school! He was not a brilliant teacher but at least was not as cruel and as addicted to drink as 'Blackbird.'

When George was twelve his father sent him to a finishing school at Blennerhasset. He was there for just three months: the cost was eight shillings, but in the boy's opinion well worth it. He recalled: "The master was a good writer and a superior man - indeed a sort of genius. For the first time I felt that there was some use in learning, and then I began to feel how ignorant I was. However I never swerved from my resolve to go away from home. I had no tastes in common with my brother. I felt that I could not hang about half idle, with no better prospect before me than that of being a farm servant, so I determined that I would leave home at thirteen and fight the battle of life for myself."

A man of his word, he was to fight the battle of life with courage, determination, sheer hard work, and never-failing kindness.

After his schooldays his father had wanted him to stay on the farm, but George was ambitious. He had served out his four-year apprenticeship with Joseph Messenger, the draper in Wigton's West Street, and now had announced his intention of going to London to seek his fortune.

The night before his departure he stayed at the Grey Goat Inn. Many years later, by a strange twist of fate, he was to die there.

The journey was hardly one of luxury. It took two days and two night's travelling before the stage coach rumbled its way down Old St Pancras Road, down Gray's Inn Lane, along Holborn and Newgate Street to eventually stop at "The Swan With Two Necks", in Lad Lane, Wood Street. He had reached the big city of his dreams and quickly found accommodation at the "Magpie and Pewter Platter".

It was typical of the young George that the day after his arrival, Good Friday, he found his way to the annual sports at Chelsea - a known gathering point for Cumbrian exiles - to take part and distinguish himself by taking third prize for wrestling.

The next day he started to seek employment, but for weeks failed to find it. Employers were reluctant to take on a country lad from Cumberland. His accent was that of the countryside, as were his simple clothes. It was the Cumbrian connection that at last found him a job with Flint, Ray and Company, a firm of retail drapers; happily, and by no coincidence, the owner of the company was a Cumberland man!

Just a few months later Eliza, his master's attractive young daughter, came tripping into the warehouse with her mother. George fell in love immediately; ever a single-minded young man, he vowed that one day she would be his wife. In 1840 she did. But not before George carved himself a name as a super salesman. He left the retail trade for a wholesale company and became their town traveller and later coverd the huge and important territories of Manchester and Liverpool. He specialised in lace goods and was a superb salesman, earning the nickname of the "Napoleon of Lace. Aged just twenty-four, he was made a partner in the firm of Groucock and Copestake.

With George's business acumen and his sales techniques the business rapidly expanded, and in 1834 the firm moved to Bow Churchyard where it remained for many years.

George Moore had a strict seven-days-a-week work regime. He could follow it thanks to good health, an iron constitution and great willpower. He usually worked sixteen hours a day, but also worked on Saturdays. On Sundays he was kept busy preparing accounts and checking the stock. On the road his personality and honesty meant that he kept his customers for life. Said a Mr Crampton, who later became his partner: "He made personal friends wherever he went, and kept them; his name was a household word over the country."

With two such travellers as Moore and Groucock, with a capable Copestake in charge of the warehouse, the firm prospered, later even opening their own lace-making factory in Nottingham. After three years he was earning a third share of the profits. "Groucock and I," said George, "extended the business so rapidly that poor Copestake was often very hard up to pay the accounts for lace. I did almost double the business of any other traveller on the road. "I laboured day and night. Our business increased every year . . . I visited every market town in England, Scotland, Ireland and Wales, with very few exceptions."

More travelling for the energetic George was needed when, with Groucock, he went on lace-buying expeditions. On these expeditions they would visit most of the towns in Belgium and France.

George Moore let nothing stand between him and his determination to succeed. It was once demonstrated when he was on a sales mission to Ireland, sailing from Plymouth to Dublin. It was a wild winter's night, a high sea was running, and the vessel in which he was to sail was anchored quite a distance offshore. He was having difficulty finding sailors willing to face the rough sea in an open boat, but eventually found enough to ferry him out to the ship. His boxes of lace were brought down from the shore and hoisted into the boat. George had with him an elderly servant to care for the boxes who was terrified. As he gazed at the heaving sea, he implored George not to risk his life and lace in the open boat. "Stop behind then," said George, "for I am determined to go!" He then sprang into the boat and it was launched. Every so often it disappeared from view as it slid into the trough of huge waves. It took an hour to reach the ship, the boatmen fighting their way through one of the wildest storms ever to break over that stretch of the rocky coast.

George Moore seemed to have a charmed life. It was certainly at risk again when, after travelling through Cumberland, he arrived at Cartmel; he was heading for Lancaster, his next port of call, and driving his own two-horse carriage carrying a large quantity of valuable lace. Unwilling as ever to lose a moment, he decided to take a short cut across the Morecambe Bay sands. He did not know how treacherous they were - over the years hundreds had been drowned attempting to cross the nine miles from Cartmel to Poulton-le-sands on the opposite shore. It was normal to have a guide - called a Carter - to take strangers across the constantly shifting sands. That was not for George Moore. Arriving shortly before evening he took no time to check the state of the tide but drove at once onto the sands. It was a reckless move, and he was to soon find out just how stupid and dangerous it was. The short cut that was to save him the fifty extra miles by going inland and round the Kent and Leven rivers was very nearly the short cut to the end of his life.

Halfway across he saw that the tide was turning. The man with him in the carriage jumped out and fled back to Cartmel. George drove on. The water, like a mill-race, was now rushing towards him at a terrifying speed. He flogged his horses as they had never been flogged before, but the wet sand gave no firm footing, he turned them to the side and drove them where their feet held, but he was losing the race with the tide. By now the water was rising rapidly; the boxes of lace behind him were already afloat. Turning this way and that way he still could find no sure foothold for the horses. Worse, confused, he was driving to destruction. He was heading for the open sea! His luck held. Suddenly he heard a shout from his left. Looking round he spotted a man on horseback shouting and waving his hands. It was one of the mounted guides, stationed on the shore to watch over the dangerous waters. The guide spurred his horse into the water and pointed the way that George should take. It was not too soon. By now his horses were swimming, but by sheer force he pulled them round and headed for the land. In desperation he flogged out of them the last ounce of energy that took them to firm ground. The exhausted horses dragged the carriage up the bank. George Moore's life was saved.

In 1841 George Moore gave up regular travelling. Instead he worked in the office and the warehouse, but because of that his health suffered. His doctor told him he was working his brain too much and his body too little.

Horse-riding as an exercise was recommended and in the winter he took to hunting two days a week; it would have come naturally to one who, as a boy, had hunted with John Peel.

The summer was spent in voluntary work, helping institutions like the Cumberland Benevolent Society. He also helped create the Commercial Travellers' School at Pinner. The school attracted the admiration of Charles Dickens who visited the school, took the chair at an anniversary dinner and used the title The Uncommercial Traveller for one of his books.

John Forster, in his biography of Dickens, says that the famous author had a great admiration for George Moore's business qualities. When Dickens wanted support for any good work his first thought was George Moore and his appeals to him were never made in vain. Dickens once told the Commercial and Travellers' Association: "Integrity, enterprise, public spirit and benevolence had their synonym in Mr Moore's name."

Dickens was ever ready to pay tribute to George Moore's generosity, but there were others who experienced it. In 1854, when he moved home from Oxford Terrace to a mansion in Kensington Palace Gardens, he arranged a splendid ball for the staff of Groucock, Copestake and Moore. Said George: "As our young men and women at Bow Churchyard had been instrumental in helping me to gain the wealth for building such a house, I determined that they should be the first to visit us.

"We gave a ball to about 300 of our own people and allowed the young men to invite their female friends to equalise the sexes. After the dancing there was a grand supper. We gave a second ball to all the porters and their wives, the drivers, and the female servants. There were about two hundred in all. We employed omnibuses to bring them to the house and send them away. They got abundant refreshment and danced to their hearts' content."

For George there must have been moments of sadness during these celebrations. His beloved wife Eliza had been ailing for a long time and was now very ill. She had suffered a great deal of pain on a journey from Shap Wells to London, and on arrival had taken to her bed where she remained for many months. Said George: "Her dreams of happiness in her new house have been sadly marred by her severe affliction. The great anxiety she went through during its building and furnishing have not been repaid; she has ceased to enjoy these splendid rooms."

Everything was done to restore her health: the best physicians and surgeons were called in and consulted, but to no avail. They declared her to be seriously ill. Eliza died on December 4, 1858. George Moore was desolate with grief. He had waited years before being able to fulfill his vow to marry her. Now she was gone. She was buried in Cumberland, laid to rest in a mausoleum in Allhallows churchyard.

A splendid monument some thirty-two feet high, featuring a memorial fountain with a pedestal of polished granite, was erected to Eliza's memory. It still stands at the end of the street in Wigton, appropriately just yards from the site of the drapers where George first served his apprenticeship. The following month George presented an organ to Wigton's church. The inscription read: "In gratitude to Almighty God, and in remembrance of early days, this organ is presented to the parish church of Wigton by George Moore, AD 1859."

George's good works were endless. He visited the new city prison at Holloway. Whilst there he asked a chaplain what became of prisoners when they completed their sentences. He was told that they would return to stealing as nobody would employ them. Said George: "I at once determined, with God's help, to establish a Reformatory for young men." With the assistance of banker friend James Cunliffe he did so, immediately taking over large premises and grounds on Brixton Hill.

But one of the most remarkable and unique ways by which George showed his benevolence was assisting in the marriage of people who were not, but who ought to have been, married. City missionaries, with whom he worked, discovered many hundreds of men and women living together without being married. Women were in a disreputable social situation, and the children were growing up illegitimate. Over a period of twenty years, to protect the women and tie them to husbands and to give the children a father's name, George paid the marriage fees of thousands. He hid his lamp of kindness under a bushel. Clergymen never discovered who paid the marriage fees; those thus married never knew their benefactor.

Through this work, and the city missionaries, he discovered one of the other hidden faces of London - the demoralisation of hundreds of women; with

The George Moore Memorial Fountain in Wigton under construction.

his friend Mr Robert Hanbury, MP., he established a refuge for fallen women.

George Moore also helped found a Home for Incurables at Carshalton. No sooner was it opened thanevery bed was full.

Another institution to earn him their thanks was the General Porters Benevolent Association. George took the chair when the association was launched on December 9, 1857. About 1,200 porters were present. He said afterwards: "A more gratifying scene I never beheld." Every year he wrote in his pocket book:

"What I spent I had:
What I saved I lost:
What I gave I have."

The George Moore Memorial Fountain in Wigton.

In 1858 the Whitehall estate, six miles south-west of Wigton and the ancient home of the Border family of the Percys, and, later, the Salkelds, was up for sale. It was close to Mealsgate where he was born, and in October George Moore bought it. There were to be four years of restoration work before he could use it, and whilst he was in London his good friend Henry Howard of Greystoke Castle helped with the planning and the supervision of the work as the ruined buildings were restored. Two hundred navvies were employed to remake the terrace and replace the bowling green, old rooms and old rafters were preserved whilst new rooms were built on old foundations. Again, when he was staying at Whitehall, his hospitality was bound-

A Victorian cartoon showing George Moore as St George slaying "the underfed dragon".

less. One day he hosted the Rifle Volunteers. Said George: "They came along the road playing a lively tune. They and the farmers, about four hundred in all, got a good hot dinner. I carved for all."

George never paused from his good works. He became a JP, sitting with the Wigton magistrates; he was at the meetings of the Archaeological Institute; he was made chairman of the Wigton Agricultural Society. In London he had been Governor and Almoner of Christ's Hospital, a Trustee of the YMCA, a trustee to the Penny Bank in Milton Street, as well as being involved with a host of other organisations.

After the death of Eliza he felt very lonely in his splendid mansion, saying: "I feel very desolate and have no one to care for me but Christ." Despite that he recovered from his loss and once again began to entertain company. The first friends he invited to his house were his old Cumberland chums living in London. They spent pleasant evenings talking over old times and canny Cumberland ways. He was a popular and generous host; sometimes there were so many staying in the house that he gave up his own bed and slept in a neighbour's house.

He still found himself lonely when visiting Whitehall. He had no wife, no children. He could only forget his sorrow by inviting more guests to dinner. "I seem to be afraid, " he said, "of being alone."

When he came home, tired with his day's work, there was no-one to cheer him, no-one to sympathise with him, no one to lean upon. No matter how faithful were the friends who dined with him, they did not light up his house with joy. When they departed and the last man had left the door, he was left alone and unhappy.

On one of his days at Whitehall he entered in his diary: "When shall my solitary state be changed?" The answer was not long coming. Some of George's friends had hinted that he should marry again if he found the right person. Some months later he did. She was Agnes, second daughter of the late Richard Breeks of Warcop, in Westmoreland. He was smitten. In his diary he described her as his 'castle in the air'. He escorted her to a private viewing of the Royal Academy, took her out on the town and visited her family. On November 21, 1861 they were married in St Pancras Church and spent their honeymoon on a four-month tour of France and Italy.

Ten years later, during the Franco-Prussian War, he was back in France. His diary read: "My heart is sick at he carnage and death which this war is now causing throughout France. We have not heard from the managers of our Paris house for two months. We do not know whether our people are dead or alive." Paris was under siege by a German army. On September 19, 1870, the net around the city tightened. In the words of the enemy General Bismarck the citizens were left to stew in their own gravy. In the city food

Whitehall, George Moore's house at Mealsgate from a contemporary painting.

15

was scarce and soon the besieged citizens were starving. All horseflesh had been eaten, dogs and cats were hard to find. Rats and mice were eagerly seized for the cooking pots. Fuel was also scarce; people stayed in bed to keep warm. Many died, and a tragic number of children were perishing. Too common a sight was that of undertakers carrying tragically small deal coffins. Adults were transported to the cemetery in handcarts. Beaten to its knees, Paris at last surrendered.

Meanwhile Alderman Dakin, the Lord Mayor of London, had been organising a relief fund. He had raised some £12,000 to be used as soon as the gates of Paris re-opened.

George Moore was an active member of the Lord Mayor's committee. He recalled: "The French distress gives me a great deal of work."

On January 28, 1871, he entered in his diary: "Thank God there is an armistice in France. I fear that I shall have to go over to distribute the Mansion House Fund. If I go it will be as an act of duty."

Three days later he wrote: "The Lord Mayor and many others made me promise to go over to Paris..."

It was 7.45am on an icy morning when George, his clerk - Colonel Wortley - and a French lady who had been separated from her husband during the siege - set off from Newhaven for Dieppe, taking with them seventy tons of food and £5,000 in cash.

On arrival at Dieppe there were no porters to help them. The locals had not heard that the siege of Paris had been lifted.

Moreover the town was occupied by the Prussians, who were controlling the railway and the public offices. At the end of the day there were still no carriages or wagons. At last the directors of the railway were found and promised a train for them the next evening. George Moore fumed at the frustrations and delays. Later he said: "I think I would have died had I not been first in Paris."

There were more obstacles. Bridges had been blown up, rails lifted, there were only temporary repairs to the line. Nevertheless the wagons carrying the food from London were the first to pass, arriving in Amiens at 6am. From that point the train was stopped at every station to be inspected by German commandants. Credentials were checked and their train was allowed to continue on its mission of mercy.

Samuel Smiles, in his biography of George Moore, told how the food convoy reached Creil at 2 p.m. "After stopping for two hours it was allowed to pass over the creaking temporary bridge, scarcely finished. Crawling along, the engine stopping, watering, and groaning away - the train at length reached Chantilly at five in the evening. There it was shunted into a siding and waited for three hours until the Grand Duke of Mecklenburg had passed in a special train." After this further delay the relief train struggled through to St Denis. At 1 p.m. it finally arrived in Paris."

George was delighted to discover that theirs was the first train to arrive with food for the beleaguered French. But again the station was deserted and in total darkness. Not a porter was in sight, the streets were empty and the city seemed to be deserted.

George and his party set off, walking the three miles to the Boulevard Malesherbes. The lady seeking her husband discovered that he had left that morning in search of her!

Another task was waiting to challenge him - that of organising the distribution of the food. Early next day George and Colonel Wortley, accompanied by M. Andree, George's French banker - who was also a deputy Mayor - paid a call on Jules Ferry at the Hotel De Vilie. It was decided that the food should be split between twenty of the most needy arrondisements. They also decided to open a central depot, and to save expense use his company's offices. The warehouse of Copestake, Moore and Company, in the Place De Petit Peres, was to become a symbol of hope for the starving population.

George discovered that the logistics of distribution were daunting. Fifty thousand horses had been eaten during the siege, those remaining were scraggy and uneatable, and used only for dragging cannons into position.

George was furious. His diary recorded: "I felt as if the lives of thousands depended upon our efforts." He called on the military's officers, finally reaching a General Vinoy who allowed some artillery horses to drag the stores from the train to the warehouse

Two days later the distribution of much-needed food started.. Crowds of desperate people gathered in the Place De Petit Peres.

Said George Moore: "Never did 1 see such an assembly of hollow, lean, hungry faces - such a shrunken, famine-stricken, diseased-looking crowd. They were very quiet. They seemed utterly crushed and hopeless. It is now ten days since the armistice began, and yet there is no food in Paris except what we have brought...

"We went about the markets. there was positively nothing to see, except a few dead dogs and cats - no flour, no vegetables. Hundreds, perhaps thousands of old people, little children, and ladies, have died of hunger. The sufferings of the little ones will never be forgotten. "For four months there was no milk, no fat except at fabulous prices, no fuel, no light. Indeed they have died in vast numbers."

The warehouse was besieged. George recalled: "There is a crowd of ten or fifteen thousand waiting there today; they have waited all through last night. I felt heartsick when I saw them. It was one of the wildest nights of sleet and fearful wind; and, starved and exhausted and drenched as they were, it was a sight to make a strong man weep.

"We are straining ourselves and all about us to the utmost. I believe we were just in time; a few days more and the people would have been too far gone; many were hardly to walk away with their parcels. After waiting with wonderful patience, when they got the food many of them fairly broke down from overjoy. I have seen more tears shed by men and women than I hope I shall ever see again."

On February 22nd, police ordered the end of distribution from the warehouse, the huge crowds were blocking the road. George said: "We put on all steam and determined to stay open all night as well as during the following day. All the streets around the warehouse were blocked with people. The food was ready for distribution. We calculated that we ran a party through in half a minute! The French people were astonished at our energy. They cheered me. I remained until one at night, and left them in full swing."

When the warehouse closed at 8 p.m. on the evening of the 23rd they had distributed food to over 96,000 persons! A grateful French government later gave George Moore, along with many others, the award of the National Order of the Legion of Honour.

Back in England another busy, though more pleasant, year awaited George Moore. In 1872 he was appointed High Sheriff of Cumberland, a term of office marked by lunches, dinners, entertainments and banquets. When the Summer Assizes were held in July High Sheriff George Moore gave a parting dinner for over 200 - barristers, magistrates and friends that included his farmers and poor relations as well as many of his Cumberland friends from London. But many of his old friends wery dying. His brother-in-law, James Willkinson Breeks died in India, aged just forty-two. Another freind to pass on was Mr Hasell, of Dalemain, near Penrith. But George Moore could not let sadness affect his charitable work. First there was the enlargement of the Convalescent Hospital at Silloth, to which, some years before, he had given £250. More important was the plan to board out pauper children. He considered that being a pauper was degrading to men and especially to children. His plan was to take children out of workhouses and bring them up in healthy homes. His diary for May 3rd, 1870, recorded that he had called on Mr Goschen, chairman of the Poor Law Board to ask for powers to board out orphan children from the Union - the workhouse.

On August 14th that year he wrote: "1 had a most satisfactory day yesterday, I was accompanied by four of the Cockermouth Guardians to board out pauper children. We placed twelve orphans with most respectable people."

It was not always the poor the needy, or the underprivileged that sparked an interest from George. At the beginning of 1874 the body of famous explorer Dr Stanley Livingstone was on its way from Zanzibar to England; his many friends in London wanted him buried at Westminster Abbey among the other great people of years past. Sadly no-one was prepared to pay the cost. Parliament were told by M.P. Russell Gurney that Stanley's family could not afford it and that the Geographical Society had no funds to spare. "The expense of interment would be very small, but there was none to whom they could look for funds except the Government; and he was quite sure that incurring the small outlay which would be required the Government would be doing an act that would be welcomed by the whole community."

But when George Moore heard of the problem he exclaimed: "Let me bury the noble dead! What! Bury him like a pauper out of the public taxes? No! Let me defray the expenses of interring the indomitable, valiant, self-denying hero!"

The Government could not allow this. The Treasury had promised £250 for the funeral. This was not enough but George's offer was still turned down. The official statement said: "A wealthy merchant in the city had offered to pay the expenses; but the Treasury felt that to accept this offer would not be in accordance with the wishes of the country."

George had the final word. He paid for the splendid tablet of black marble with its long inscription which lies over the grave of the famous explorer, the only memorial to him in the Abbey. George Moore never forgot his early days in London as a raw lad from the north with simple clothing and a Cumberland accent and never failed to help others in the same situation. He secured jobs for hundreds of young men in London. He wrote: "It is remarkable the number of Cumberland young men who call on me every day. I certainly engage a great many and those I cannot engage I try to get situations for. Today one called who had served his apprenticeship at Wigton. He said that he had been in London for one month, and must return next week as his money was nearly done. Then he burst into tears. I sent him up to get his dinner. When he came down I gave him a letter to a house that might possibly engage him. I cheered him up by promising him a dinner every day until I succeeded. Another, from Penrith, has just come in, under similar circumstances!"

The first Christmas and the last which George Moore spent in Cumberland since he was a boy, was in 1875. He wanted an old-fashioned Christmas Day, inviting all his nearest relations to Whitehall, after dinner sitting around the fire recalling their young days and recalling their Christmas Days of the past. They all claimed that there were none like the old days. George Moore sprang up and stood in front of the fire. "Yes", he said, "we all cling to the old customs. There are no mince pies like those I had when I was a boy! There are no old folks nights, no young folks nights. Yes, we are getting too old for that..."

On New Year's eve Mr and Mrs Moore entertained one hundred and seventy-five guests, those staying in the house were joined by neighbours, the workers, their children and the servants. All were given Christmas presents. There were games and dances in the hall and the night ended with everyone on the floor for the favourite country dance, Sir Roger De Coverley.

George Moore ended his diary for that year with the words: "Where shall I be this day next year? I hope I shall be better prepared to die."

He was not to see another Christmas. And no-one was prepared for the shock of his sudden death. But George Moore must have had a premonition of death.

On his last Sunday at Whitehall he attended morning service at Allhallows Church. As he went down the garden he called the faithful Potter to him and said, "Be sure to look after the poor people when I have gone."

The next day a meeting was to be held in Carlisle to discuss a plans for a Nurses Home. Mrs Moore, a member of the committee, was due to attend, but George had an appointment in Aspatria. Early on that Monday morning he turned to his wife and said: "I have been thinking about that Nurses Home and I think I ought to go. I felt no interest about as long as I thought it was only to have nurses for the rich, but now it is different."

Mrs Moore tried to dissuade him. At breakfast he said: "I must go; it will be the last time I shall be in Carlisle."

"Don't talk nonsense", replied his wife. "What do you mean?"

"Replied George: "I mean that I shall never be on a platform there again."

Their carriage was now at the door. Before entering it George called to his wife, descending the stairs: "What is that passage in St Matthew?"

"Do you mean 'I was sick and you visited me?'"

"No", he said, "I remember: 'Well done thou good and faithful servant, enter thou into the joy of thy Lord.'" They were the last words that passed between husband and wife in their happy home.

They drove off to the station, catching a train that arrived in Carlisle at mid-day. The meeting was scheduled for 2 p.m. At about 1.30 p.m., while Mrs Moore and her sister went shopping, George and Mr James Steel, owner and Editor of the Carlisle Journal, made their way down English Street. They were standing opposite the Grey Goat Inn when two runaway horses that had escaped from a livery stable in Lonsdale Street galloped past at a furious pace. Mr Steel had crossed the road and was on the pavement when the first of the two horses clattered between George Moore and himself. The other horse, just a few yards behind, was upon George in seconds. He tried to step out of the way, but it was too late. He was hit by the horse and knocked down, falling on his right side with his head and shoulders crashing to the ground.

Unconscious, he was carried into the Grey Goat Inn. Four of his ribs were broken, one puncturing his lung, his collar bone was broken, his head was severely bruised, he was suffering severe nervous shock, had difficulty breathing and complained of a severe pain in the back. Meanwhile Mrs Moore had been waiting at the Town Hall where the meeting was to have been held. Later she said: "Dr Barnes came up to me looking very pale, and said: "Mrs Moore, I want to speak to you."

I replied: "Is there anything wrong?"

"Mr Moore has had a little accident and is asking for you. "Dr Barnes took her to the Grey Goat Inn where she could hear George calling out loudly "Wife, wife, where's my wife?"

"When I was admitted to the room he kept on saying: 'My wife would take me from these men if she would come.' He did not recognise me at first. He knew my voice and kept saying 'I hear her voice, why does she not come?'"

"Then, thank God, a conscious look came into his eyes at last, and then he knew that I was with him."

The doctors knew there was no hope. A specialist, Sir William Gull, was called in. With Mr Copestake they arrived at four in the morning.

Said Mrs Moore: "By that time he had become colder, his breathing was very laboured. I began to have no hope. He could not speak much, it was cruel to ask him a question." Sir William Gull and Mrs Moore sat by George's bed from nine until midnight. George was conscious, recognising his sister and his old servants.

Said Mrs Moore: "By and by the terrible laboured breathing grew quieter. He was fast nearing the end of earthly life."

Crowds had blocked the road outside the Grey Goat all night. Police were called to keep them quiet and away from the window of the room where George Moore lay. He died at twenty minutes to two on the afternoon of November 21, 1876. There were tributes by the hundred. In Silloth bells in his memory were placed in the church; Wigton's church had a beautiful window, his employees in London raised £500 and presented a boat to the National Lifeboat Institute. It was stationed on the wild and rocky coast of Caernavonshire. The first call-out of "The George Moore Memorial Lifeboat" saw the rescue of the crew of the schooner Velocity - sailing out of Silloth!

The citizens of Paris remembered the man who saved them from

The George Moore window in St Mary's Church, Wigton.

starving. A marble tablet with a medallion showing his face was placed in Carlisle Cathedral. The epitaph was composed by the Bishop of Carlisle, who, a few days after George Moore's death, preached a sermon, scarcely able to speak for tears. He said: "We have lost one who, according to human estimate, we could least afford to lose; an earnest-hearted servant of the Lord Jesus, who devoted his clear head, his mighty energies, and the princely wealth which, by his own power and industry and God's blessing on them, he had earned, to the furtherance of godliness and to the welfare of his brethren; a man standing almost by himself - at least I never saw anyone like him; a man whom all will miss, from the very highest to the very lowest; a man whose place it seems impossible to fill, a man, I may add, concerning whom it is the least necessary I should say much, because all here knew him well. Yes, George Moore has been taken from us! He rests from his labours, and his works do follow him; and he leaves us all the noblest and best of legacies - the memory of a holy life and the precious possession of a good example."

The world had lost a great and kindly man, the poor and needy had lost a benefactor, Cumberland had lost one of its finest sons.

JOHN LOSH

The Soldier from Wreay

High overhead the Indian sun blazed down on Bangalore. In a back alley its stray rays briefly picked out the movement of furtive figures slipping between the shadows of the rundown buildings. Some were fakirs, wandering beggars professing the Hindu religion. Waiting for them in a secluded back room was Said Tippal, a Drill Sergeant in the Indian Army. With him was a wizened old button-maker from Hyderabad, but who had for years been a resident of Bangalore. Wreathes of opium smoke curled above the heads of the group. They were conspirators. Their brains fogged by drugs and alcohol. They were plotting mutiny. Their objective, to kick the British out of India. They were to be foiled by a son of a Cumbrian who was the hero of a tale that could have come straight out of The Arabian Nights. Fluent in many native dialects, he wandered the market places and alleys of Bangalore to uncover a plot that threatened bloodshed and was a serious threat to British rule in the India of 1832.

He was John Losh, eldest son of Newcastle barrister James Losh, and grandson of John Losh, who lived at Woodside, the estate some three miles south of Carlisle.

Serving in the army he proved to be a brilliant student of Indian dialects, passing examinations in eight of the native languages. A senior officer once described him as "an extraordinary young man, certainly the best linguist in the Madras Army."

He eventually became Military Auditor General of Madras, but it was as a younger officer, a Lieutenant of the 9th regiment of Madras Infantry, that he first made his name. His adventures started when the Indian Government took possession of the Kingdom of Mysore, and ended the authority of the Rajah.

The Grave of John Losh in Wreay Churchyard.

It had created discontent among the inhabitants, particularly those formerly employed by the Hindu Government. John, writing to his father, told him: "In addition to this a considerable part of the Rajah's army had been disbanded and the discharged men (principally turbulent and dissipated Mussulmen) were thrown upon the world without support and naturally resorted to the large town of Bangalore as the most likely place to find employment.

"There was, in consequence, an abundant supply of inflammable materials for a disturbance of any kind, and this circumstance was taken advantage of by some designing persons who had little to hope for under the present system, and whose chance of obtaining power or wealth rested in the prospect of change of some kind or the other.."

The year before the Muslim population had been showing signs of discontent. Said Lieutenant John Losh: "It was evident that this feeling would display itself in some attempt at a rising, or other outbreak, shortly.

"About the middle of last year, at the commencement of the great Mussulman festival of the Muhurrum, the greater part of the Mohammedan population of Bangalore, proceeding in procession to their Mesjid (Mosque) which stood about a mile from the town, discovered a pig with its throat cut and cleaned in the European fashion, which had evidently been placed there a short time before. This appearance caused, of course, a violent excitement in the crowd, and immediately a cry was raised that the deed had been done by the Missionaries, who are very numerous at Bangalore.

"The rage of the excited mob was thus turned against the Christians, and they returned towards the town for the purpose of destroying the chapels and other places of worship. However, the congregation at the first chapel before which they arrived made a stout resistance, and after a scuffle and tumult, in which little damage was done, the creators of mischief on this occasion found that their plan had failed completely, as the native troops took little share in the affair and behaved as well as possible when ordered to act.

"The mob, after throwing some volleys of stones by which several officers and some of the Christian Missionaries were hurt, dispersed, and very active and unceasing enquiries were made for some time without success regarding the origin of this affair.

"At length the killer of the pig was betrayed by his accomplices, and on being interrogated, declared that he was bribed to the act by the Colonel who commanded Bangalore and another officer at the head of the Police Department.

"As these officers were both of the class called here 'moonlighters' whose chief business is vain attempts to convert the Indians, the story of the detected incendiary was believed by the ignorant multitude, who became more than ever excited against the Christians; tho' the Government took great pains to undermine them, and even built a new Mesjid at a very considerable expense - the former one being defiled by the dead pig."

Bangalore was not the only town to be so affected. Bellary, Cuddapah, Azeph and Pawlgardcherry, all military stations, saw similar disturbances. In each the same means were used, a dead pig left in the mosque inciting more violent reaction. John Losh reported: " At Cuddapah the mob were fired upon, and the collector and Magistrate, a Mr McDonald, were stabbed while addressing the crowd, several sepoys were also killed."

In September the leader of the Bangalore pig plot, a sepoy in one of the Native Regiments, was charged with inciting mutiny. He was shot, but died like a martyr, threatening to return in the shape of the devil and take revenge on the Christians of Mysore. Those who killed the pigs at the other stations were not discovered.

Lieutenant Losh reported: "The planners of the second plot appear to be some fakirs and a native of Hyderabad, who was a button maker and was for many years resident at Bangalore."

India was a world in which many believed in strange omens, prophecies and predictions. It was no surprise then that the conspirators dreamed up and spread a tale that said a great saint had arrived at Bangalore who could convert base metals into gold, the precious metal so produced was to be used to promote the Hindu religion.

Said Losh: " Many of the native soldiers were then induced to attend a meeting of the conspirators, and amongst the rest the Drill Halvidar of my regiment, who afterwards took so prominent a part in the plot he was considered the ringleader, and, to the last, declared that he had seen gold made repeatedly and in large quantities.

"After a short time these meetings were more numerously attended, and the plot was communicated to visitors to whom liquor, opium and other intoxicating drugs were distributed in abundance. About twenty of the native troops at Bangalore were acquainted with the particulars of the plan, and many more, no doubt, were aware that something was in agitation and would have lent them assistance had they seen a probability of success..

"The other conspirators who have been discovered are in number about 150, and this appeared to have been the whole force on which the ringleaders could depend. They, of course, reckoned on the rising of the whole native population of Bangalore, which is very great."

Losh uncovered more details of the planned mutiny: "Many papers were prepared for circulation, calling on all people to arm for the defence of the true religion, and flags and standards, with pom-poms and inscriptions in Persian, were kept in readiness.

"The plan was as follows. The Drill Halvidar of the 9th Regiment, whose name was Said Tippas, and who, from the time of his joining the party, was considered by all as the chief, was to enter the fort with about fifty men and there to overpower the English soldiers at the Main Guard, secure the arsenal and murder the General and his family who resided in the fort. . . "

Lieutenant Losh revealed more details. The mutineers planned even more bloodshed. Once the fort was taken a signal was to be made by firing a gun from the ramparts. Those waiting in the cantonments would then attack and take the barracks of the 9th Regiment, arm themselves, to then secure the other barracks and murder all officers - European and native, English Cavalry - as well as an infantry regiment with two companies of artillery and all the loyal native troops, among whom were some 4,000 Hindus.

A wild plan. Said Losh: "How these people intended the dispatch of the English troops in the barracks it is difficult to conceive, though they declared to the last that their plan was to bring the guns from the Horse Artillery park and fire them into the barracks till the inmates were exterminated.

"All the officers and soldiers having been murdered the conspirators had determined to divide the ladies, and other European women, among themselves by lots. It was thought at first that their plan was to keep them as hostages, but it appears that the wretched people had not sense sufficient to hit on this plan - and no doubt the treatment of the women would have been horrible."

The plotters had been ambitious. Having succeeded the old button maker was to be proclaimed Regent of Mysore. Said Tippal, the Halvidar, was to be his Prime Minister and Commander-inchief of a force which was to advance upon Madras and deliver the country from English domination.

Said Losh: " Altogether a more wicked, insane and impracticable plan was never thought of or intended to be carried into execution, yet, ridiculous as it now appears, there is little doubt that had the villains made any attempt the mischief and loss of life would have been exceedingly great.

"The fort is four miles from the cantonments, and was defended merely by a guard of about twenty soldiers who were posted at the principal gate, the other gate was guarded by about an equal number of natives, and these guards were sent daily from the cantonment. "On the morning of the day on which the rising was to have taken place the conspirators contrived to get one of their number placed at the Mysore gate of the fort so that their entrance was secured at any time that suited them.

"The attack was to have commenced at 11 o'clock a.m. - at 3a.m. the whole plan had been disclosed by a Hindu who had been long in appearance a partner in the plan, and before 6 most of the mutineers had been seized and the fort and town, as well as the cantonment, were occupied by strong parties of European forces."

Punishment was swift - and bloody. Six of the conspirators were executed on December 24th, four of them by being tied to the mouths of cannon and blown to pieces. Two others were shot by a firing squad.

Lieutenant Losh described the scene: "The whole of a very large force stationed at Bangalore was out on this occasion and formed three sides of a square, the fourth being occupied by the guns and the Horse Artillery and the Sepoys selected to shoot the prisoners. "The criminals behaved very firmly, kissing the guns before being fastened to them. On the firing of the guns the four black heads rose some yards above the smoke, and fell exactly in front of the guns from which they had risen. The arms and the whole of the upper part of the prisoners were blown to pieces and scattered in various directions, some fragments falling amongst the troops on the arms of the square.

"Altogether the spectacle was disgusting, tho' the criminals, in fact, must have suffered less than if they had been hung.

Wreay Syke, the house in Wreay where John Losh spent his last years.

"The business took up a long time, and the excessive heat of the day, the might of the arms, and the sight of the mangled bodies covered by hordes of vultures and kites rendered the transaction anything but pleasant to the spectators.

"Such was the finishing scene of the most wicked and infamous plot, which, ridiculous as it now appears to have been, gave the Authorities a fright from which they did not for some time recover.

His task completed Lieutenant Losh went back to his studies. He ended his report: "After the prisoners were disposed of there was no reason for detaining me any longer at Bangalore, and on the 14th January I obtained leave to return to Madras to finish my studies previous to the Pilosoo Examination."

John Losh proved to be an extremely able officer, eventually promoted Military Auditor General of Madras. He later retired from the army to live in Wreay Syke where he died in 1861 and was buried in the family plot in the village churchyard.

Jonathan Boucher

JONATHAN BOUCHER

The Preacher Friend of Washington from Blencogo

A boy born in a small Cumbrian village was destined to leave behind the rural life, cross the Atlantic to live in Virginia. There he became a neighbour and friend of George Washington, one of the prime movers of the revolution of 1776. Their friendship only ended by the following American War of Independence and Washington's part in it.

He was Jonathan Boucher. In 1755, as a young man, he was finding life pleasant enough. It was a Friday and he was listening to the scholars of St Bees school reciting their lessons of the week. Only a few months earlier the Cumberland lad had been studying mathematics, navigation and land surveying under Isaac Ritson. Ritson, who was from Workington, was a shoe-maker by trade. He became a self-taught mathematician and, at the age of forty, he took holy orders to become Minister of a chapel at Clifton. He was also the town's schoolmaster and the local surveyor.

Jonathan was born on March 1, 1737, at Blencogo, in the parish of Bromfield, a son of a family that for centuries had been wealthy land-owners but, as the years passed, the estates had been frittered away.

Jonathan's father, James Boucher, had married again after the death of Eleanor, his first wife. His new bride was Anne Barnes, daughter of a weaver, said to be a coarse woman of low taste but with the saving grace of being an energetic housewife. It was Anne who persuaded husband James to become the village schoolmaster and, fatefully, also to open an ale-house. The couple had four children, John, born in 1734, Mary, born in 1736, Jonathan, who had followed a year later, and their youngest child, Jane, who arrived in 1741. Of the four, Jonathan and Jane were to become the closest, living most of their lives together.

Jonathan's early days were unhappy ones, spent in horrendous poverty. His father was his own best customer at the ale-house. In later years Jonathan recalled living in "a state of penury and hardship as I have never seen since equalled, no, not even in parish almshouses." Despite his addiction to drink, James did find time to teach his son to read, and when the boy, at the age of six, became a pupil at the small free school in Bromfield he could already read and spell very well.

He studied Latin with a Mr Lowther, a dedicated teacher who all too soon disappeared to be replaced by others who were indifferent. The poor standard of teaching, allied to Jonathan's frequent absences caused by the family's need for labour, led to a hit-or-miss education, but opportunity was waiting in the wings.

In Wigton, the nearby market town, there was a school that prepared students to become teachers. For quite a time the young Jonathan walked the four miles to and from Wigton to be tutored there by the Reverend Joseph Blain. In 1754, just sixteen years old, Jonathan qualified as a schoolteacher.

He turned down posts at Crookdake and Raughtonhead, choosing instead to accept one in Wigton. There he taught thirty-two boys who each paid him ten shillings a year. But he was an ambitious young man, determined to become a man of letters, a determination that led to his decision to move and study under the Ritsons at Workington.

It was to be no bed of roses. Life with the Ritsons was one of frugality and self-discipline. Jonathan recalled: "For a month or more I was surveying land every day, and in very severe weather, we worked from sun to sun without eating or drinking and I do not remember ever to have dined at his house when there was not salmon and potatoes mashed, or when there was anything else . . . "

Jonathan, keen to further his literary ambitions, considered going to Ireland. His father had other ideas. He ordered his son to apply for an ushership at St Bees, where, as such, he would assist the schoolmaster and board with the family.

It was a reluctant Jonathan that walked the ten miles from Workington to St Bees, but it was to be the turning point in his life.

John James, Rector of St Bees and the master of the boys' free grammar school, was taken aback by the new usher's lack of grammar.

Despite that, he wisely recognised some potential in the young man. Jonathan was accepted and moved in with John James. Soon afterwards Mr James married Ann Grayson and the usher found himself living a life in complete contrast to the harsh regime of the Ritsons. Jonathan was to share in the warmth and pleasure of a loving and close-knit family, John James was destined to become the man who exercised most influence over him. During the fifteen years he was to spend in America Jonathan sent regular letters home to his old tutor and friend.

John James had taught him well. Years later Jonathan's grandson - another Jonathan - said of him: "No threats or dangers could make him flinch for a single moment from doing what he believed to be his duty; and had his lot been cast in Paris in the French, instead of in Maryland in the American Revolution, I am satisfied that he would have defied Fouquier Tinsville to his face and have gone to the guillotine quite cheerfully an hour later."

The daily routine of St Bees was hard; but equally rewarding. John James had only recently taken over the school and both he and Jonathan desired to make a success of the declining and badly managed institution.

They rose at six and ceased work only when it was too dark to see. Within two years their endeavours were rewarded; the total of pupils had reached eighty and more were enrolling. Jonathan earned ten pounds in his first year. Iin the second his annual salary was £30. But there were greater benefits, those of an education provided daily. Every day John James first went over the lesson with him, Jonathan, in turn, taught the boys in his class. Friday was repetition day when the head changed places with his usher to give Jonathan the chance to hear the higher classes recite. On Thursday nights John James listened as Jonathan read through the week's work. Three years passed, but then life at St Bees was to end. John Younger, a Whitehaven merchant acting as agent for his factor in Virginia, was seeking a young man willing to travel to the colony and become a private tutor.

He would receive £60 a year for teaching four boys and there was provision for taking on four extra pupils, with the tutor dictating his own terms. Younger would pay for the passage to America.

It was a chance too good to turn down. Jonathan accepted. He borrowed £30 with which to buy his wardrobe, and in March 1759 left Whitehaven as a passenger in the "Rose", bound for Virginia. He could never have envisaged the adventures and dramas waiting in the land 3,000 miles away. Not only was he to become the tutor to the young gentlemen of the tobacco-rich colony, he was to become neighbour, intimate friend and yet, later, a most severe critic of George Washington, victorious general in the war of Independence and later first President of the United States.

On April 12th, 1759, he stepped ashore on the banks of the Rappahannock River. He then travelled 80 miles upriver to Port Royal where he found the home of Captain Edward Dixon, father of his prospective pupils. Jonathan was twenty-one, in debt, and very much alone among people he found alien to him in manners and way of life.

It was as a tutor that he first make contact with George Washington. He later recalled: "Among my boys I had the son-in-law (sic: he meant stepson) of the since so celebrated General Washington; and this laid the foundation of a very particular intimacy and friendship which lasted till we parted, never to meet again, on our taking sides in the late struggles.

"Mr Washington was the second of five sons of parents distinguished neither for their rank or their fortune. Laurence, their eldest, became a soldier and went on the expedition to Carthagena, where, getting into some scrape with another officer, it was said that he did not acquit himself so well as he ought, and so sold out, soon after which he died at Barbadoes.

"George, who, like most people thereabouts at that time, had no other education other than reading, writing and accounts, which he was taught by a convict servant who his father bought for a schoolmaster, first set out as Surveyor of Orange County . . .

"When the French made encroachments on our western frontier in 1754, this Washington was sent out to examine on the spot how far what was alleged was true . . ."

Later, when a regiment was raised in Virginia, he was appointed Lieutenant Colonel. Said Jonathan: "I believe, at first, he was the Major only."

"I did know Mr Washington well; and though occasions may call forth traits of character that could never have been discovered in the more sequestered scenes of life, 1 cannot conceive how he could, otherwise than through the interested representations of party, have ever been spoken of as a great man.

"He is shy, silent, stern, slow and cautious, but has no quickness of parts, extraordinary penetration, nor an elevated style of thinkirg

"In his moral character he is regular, temperate, strictly just and honest (excepting as a Virginian he has lately found out there is no moral turpitude in not paying what he confesses he owes to a British creditor) and, as I always thought, religious; having hereto been pretty constant, and even exemplary in his attendance on public worship in the Church of England. But he seems to have nothing generous or affectionate in his nature. Just before the close of the last war he married the widow Custie, and thus came into the possession of her large jointure. "He never had any children, and lived very much like a gentleman at Mount Vernon, in Fairfax County, where the most distinguished part of his character was that he was an admirable farmer."

Weary of the classroom and teaching Captain Dixon's boys Jonathan cast around for a new career, and it was soon suggested that he take holy orders. The parish of Hanover had fallen vacant and the Vestry recommended Jonathan to the Bishop of London for ordination. Ordination could only be performed by a bishop and there was no Anglican bishop resident in America. It meant a voyage home.

On December 15th, 1761, Jonathan Boucher sailed for England in the aptly-named "Christian". A strange twist of fate saw him waving to another ship just in from England. Standing on deck was his sister Jinny, who, after trying her fortune in London, had decided to join her brother in America. Jonathan knew she was coming and had arranged accommodation for her with a local family until he returned.

On January 17th, 1762, after a fast but stormy passage, he arrived back in England. On March 26th he was inducted as Deacon of the Anglican church by the Right Reverend Richard Osbaldeston. Five days later he was ordained priest.

He could not have been blamed if he had nursed just one small doubt - over the years eleven ministers destined for American parishes had lost their lives during the Atlantic crossing! Before leaving Jonathan made a pilgrimage to Blencogo to bid farewell to his family. He was never to see them again. During the next few years both his parents died.

In May he once more sailed for America. On July 12th 1762 he again

Jonathan Boucher's pulpit

landed at Urbanna on the Rappahannock. It was exactly three years and three months to the day when he had first set foot in Virginia.

But by now the clouds of war were gathering. Independence from England was on everyone's lips. Never afraid to speak up against it was loyal King's man and churchman Jonathan Boucher.

In his autobiography he told the tales of troubled days. "Annapolis, to which I afterwards removed, was quite a new scene to me. It was then the genteelest town in North America, the residence of the Governor and all the great officers of state. . . The first transaction of any moment in which I engaged was the assistance I gave in a convention of the clergy of the Province, in which, chiefly through my instigation, we petitioned for a Bishop. This gave great offence, and for some time neither the Governor,

nor other influential men, would speak to me.

"Conscious only of having done my duty, I would, however, make no concessions, and I declared that however much I might be bound to them in gratitude for past favours, I would allow no man to dictate to me.

"The times had now become beyond measure troublesome; men's minds restless and dissatisfied, grumbling at the present state of things and forever projecting reformations."

The Reverend Boucher had a second tale of woe: "Queen Anne's parish in St George's County now falling vacant the Government offered it to me. It was in a healthy part of the county, I did not, therefore, hesitate to accept the living.

"On going to it I had indeed a most unpleasant reception, for the unpopular part I had lately taken respecting government had set the people against me, and they were, in general, a set of violent patriots. Hence the first Sunday I found the church doors shut against me; and not long after a turbulent fellow paid eight dollars for so many loads of stones to drive off me and my friends from church by force.

"All these difficulties only made me take more pains; and though I never made the least concession respecting my principles or conduct, I soon made a little party among them, and went on with tolerable quiet, though never with much comfort."

Jonathan was married in June, 1772. He recalled: "In a short time my wife accompanied me to my house, twenty miles from her mother's, and here we sat down to the business of life with a resolution to do our duty to the best of our power and be happy. But alas! The times grew dreadfully uneasy, and I was neither an unconcerned or idle spectator of the mischiefs that were gathering.

In the pulpit Jonathan did not lose the courage of his convictions: "I endeavoured in my sermons to check the mischief that was impending, but in vain. I received letters threatening me with the most dreadful consequences if I did not desist from preaching at all . . .

"Sometime after a public fast was ordained, and on this occasion my Curate, who was a strong republican, had prepared a sermon for the occasion, and, supported by a set of factious men, was determined to oppose my entering my own pulpit.

"When the day came I was at my church at least a quarter of an hour before the time of beginning; but, behold, Mr Harrison was in the desk, and was expected, I was soon told, to preach.

"In addition to this I saw my church filled with not less tharn two hundred armed men under the command of a Mr Osborn Sprigg, who soon told me I was not to preach..."

Jonathan could expect no help from George Washington, despite the intimate friendship of the earlier years.

Washington was by now the Commander of the Continental armies. Boucher recorded his last meeting with the man who one day would he America's, first president, saying: "I happened to be going across the Potomac with my wife and some other friends, exactly at the time that General Washington was crossing it on his way to the northward, whither he was to take command of the Continental army. There had been a great meeting of people and great doings in Alexandria on the occasion; and everybody seemed to be on fire, either with rum, or patriotism, or both- Some patriots in our boat huzzahed and gave three cheers to the General as he passed us, whilst Mr Addison and myself contented ourselves by pulling off our hats.

"The General, then only Colonel Washington, beckoned us to stop, as we did, just, as he said, to shake us by the hand.

"His behaviour to me was now, as it had always been, polite and respectful; and I shall for ever remember what passed in the few disturbed moments of conversation we then had.

"From his going on his present errand, I foresaw and apprised him of much that has since happened; in particular that there would be a civil war, and that the Americans would soon declare for independency.

With more earnestness than was usuaal with his great reserve he scouted my apprehensions, adding, and, I believe with, perfect sincerity, that if I ever heard of him joining in such measures I had his leave to set him down for everything wicked."

"This was the last time I saw this gentleman, who, contrary to all reasonable expectation, has since so distinguished himself that he will probably be handed down to posterity as one of the first characters of the age."

In June, 1776, Jonathan began to think of retreat to England. He would have to act quickly, for the Continental Congress - the thirteen states ready to sign the Declaration of Independence - had already set September 10 as the date for ending all trade and shipping with Great Britain. On August 6, 1775, he penned his last letter to George, Washington, renouncing their friendship, denouncing the patriot cause. His grandson later described it as: "...the natural outpouring of grief, indignation and disgust by a man who considered himself wrongly persecuted on account of his political opinions."

Jonathan had not held back his anger, declaring: "You are no longer worthy of my friendship; a man of honour can no longer, without d}ssst}ssoi'sT, be connected with you. With your cause renounce you."

Jonathan Boucher could stay no longer in America. In mid-August he rode into Annapolis to make arrangements, for their passage home. Nelly, his wife, at first considered staving, but anguished over 'the prospect of a long parting from her husband. On the other hand going to England with him meant leaving her family, leaving their property and living in a country foreign tco her.

All departure plans had to be completed in a week. Governor Eden gave Jonathan a letter to the Bishop of Bangor, Eden's brother-in-law, and one to the Bishop of London. His sister .lane chose to stay in America.

To protect their property friends advised Jonathan to, create the impression that he would be returning soon. The Bouchers took none of their effects with them, even leaving clothing behind. Dawn broke on the Sunday morning and the sad moment of departure had arrived arrived, Jonathan had no time to go to bed. On August 14, 1775 the exiles-to-be left their home - The Lodge - and to the weeping and sobbing of their slaves set off to board the schooner "Nell Gwynn" which would ferry them out to the frigate "Choptank", lying in the Potomac River off Quantico.

The short voyage in the schooner was miserable one. Exhausted, they slept on a bunker covered by a piece of old sail and using a small bag of Hominy as a pillow.. A day and one long night later they carne alongside the "Choptank", which, after dropping down river to the mouth of the Potomac, lingered a few days before setting -sail for the English port of Dover. On September 20, 1774; straining his eves, for a last glimpse of the sunset on what he described as a"charmingly fine evening", Jonathan lost sight of the

41

capes of Virginia, never again to see them. It was exactly sixteen years and two months since he, as a stranger seeking a new life, had first caught sight of the American shore.

Twenty years later, now living in Epsom, in Surrey, he was reconciled with Washington, dedicating his account of the War of Independence to him.

He wrote: " I was once your neighbour and friend; the, unhappy dispute which terminated in the disunion of our respective countries, also broke off our personal connexion, but I was never more than your political enemy, and every sentiment, even of political animosity, has, on my part, long ago subsided.

"Permit me then to hope that this tender of a new amity beytween us may be received and regarded as giving some promise of that perfect reconciliation between our two countries which is the sincere aim of this publication to promote."

The Reverend Boucher certainly left his mark in America. Recalling his days a sthe Rector of ST. Anne's, in Annapolis, he wrote: "I have in my custody a certificate by which it appears that on the 24th November, 1775, I baptised in St Mary's Church one hundred and fifteen negro adults, and on the 31st March, 1776, being Easter Monday, I baptised three hundred and thirteen Negro adults and lectured extempore to upwards of a thousand."

Jonathan was inordinately proud of his achievement, saying, I question whether so extraordinary an accession to the church of Chrst, by one man and in one day, can be paralleled even in the journals of a Popish missionary."

Not so bad a record for a lad from Blencogo!

42

THE DUKE OF NORFOLK

The Convivial Aristocrat from Greystoke

Just over 200 years ago a man born near Penrith was attending a huge banquet in London. He raised his glass and proposed a toast.

Normally it would have been nothing out of the usual. But this man was the Duke of Norfolk and the toast was more than unusual - it was treasonable!

The Duke, despite his royal connections, was a democrat at heart. His toast, in 1798, was to "Our sovereign's health - the majesty of the people"!

Eight words that had severe repercussions. Insulted and appalled, George III stripped the Duke of his rank of Colonel of the Militia and took away his appointment as a Lord Lieutenant.

Ironically the Duke heard the news as he was entertaining the king's son, the Prince Regent, at Norfolk House.

But then the Duke was no ordinary member of the peerage. At Arundel Castle, in Sussex, still the seat of the Dukes of Norfolk, he was said to "keep up the most magnificent state, but in town would dine at a chophouse where, from his convivial qualities, he was known as the Social Duke."

Charles Howard, the earl of Surrey - son of the 10th duke - was born in March, 1746 and brought up in Greystoke Castle. He later he was to become the most eccentric MP ever to represent Carlisle.

He spent much of his youth in France, but despite receiving little education from his tutors, both abroad and in Greystoke, was said to have a natural ability and rude eloquence. He grew up to become a large, muscular and clumsy person, and inherited the Dukedom on September 20, 1777.

Campaigning with John Christian Curwen - MP for Workington - he

The Duke of Norfolk.
Reproduced by kind permission of his Grace the Duke of Norfolk.

wrested Carlisle from the political grasp of the Lowthers. It was certainly a time of political chicanery. As early as 1756 Sir James Lowther had an income of £45,000 a year, and could spend a huge amount to make sure he was not opposed at election time. In 1778 came the most scandalous of the intrigues. In those days only freemen of the city could vote, and between September, 1784 and February, 1785, Carlisle's mayor, Jeremiah Wherling, a political puppet in the pocket of the Lowthers, allowed almost 1,500 coal-miners, employed in Sir James' pits in West Cumberland, to be admitted as freemen, thus ensuring a 'yellow' victory in 1788. Later the Duke was to expose the scandal and reveal the secret of the colaminer freemen.

If the Lowthers were detested, the Earl of Surrey was popular in Carlisle. He raced his horses on the city's course on The Swifts and was hailed as one of the most remarkable county gentlemen ever connected with Cumberland.

He certainly appeared to have a great affection for the North, and spent much of his time at Greystoke. Many odd tales were told of all-night drinking sessions whilst rain dripped through the dilapidated roof of the old castle.

The Duke was a heavy drinker - as were many uppercrust gentlemen of the time. Confirmation could be found in his diary for January 1, 1790:

"At Hereford, a dinner given by Mr R. Phillips as is customary for every person introduced into the Corporation. A large party. Very jovial. Sat late, was informed the next day that in going home I had some falls in the street that were very dangerous, but as I did not find any bad consequences, I apprehend that those who attended to take care of me were not very nice judges of danger..."

His diary for May 31 read: "Messrs Dacre and Losh came to Greystoke, drank free. .."

On July 20 he entered: "Messrs Story and Gass dined at Greystoke, all got drunk." Drunk or sober, he kept a keen eye on the political corruption by the local Tories. He had not forgotten the contrived 'yellow' victory, and on September 26, 1789, wrote: "Went to Carlisle with Mr Addison to take affidavits of old freemen and members of the Corporation to make a case against Lord Lonsdale's newly created freemen in our road." The Duke was not a devoted follower of fashion, far from it. At a time when hair-powder and

45

a queue were in vogue he wore his hair cut short and used powder only when going to court.

He was a man who with pleasure entered in his diary: "Sat first time for my picture to Hamilton - in character of King Solomon". Not so pleased on November 26, 1798, he recorded: "Dined with Mr Huddleston, came to Cockermouth at night, ordered post horses at the King's Arms - only a pair at home. Copeland, who keeps The Globe, when applied to for a pair to put to them, with great insolence said that unless I would take the four I should have none. Got a pair from Fisher, of the Golden Lion..."

It was at London's Crown and Anchor tavern, on January 24, 1798, that he proposed the infamous toast that so upset King George III. There were many guests at the great political dinner held at the tavern renowned as a regular meeting place for English republicans. One of them, Home Tooke, later tried for treason, once took the chair to denounce the aristocracy.

The Duke's rebel streak also showed in his attitude to fashion. It was said: "In his dress he was so slovenly that on one occasion he created immense excitement by appearing in the House of Lords wearing a new coat."

His choice of lady friends was unusual, too. In 1816 the Carlisle Patriot reported : "In his admiration for the fair sex the Duke had a peculiar taste; though short in stature himself his admiration never descended below 5 feet 10 inches. Thus was his scale of excellence and every female above six feet would be sure to receive the tribute of his admiration."

The noble lord also left a lot to be desired in personal hygiene. Said Cumbrian historian Dr Henry Lonsdale: "The Duke rarely made use of water for the puposes of bodily refreshment, and the servants of His Grace availed themselves of his fits of intoxication to wash their master. On these occasions they stripped him as they would have done a corpse and performed on his body the necessary ablutions." At one time he complained of his rheumatism to fellow MP Dudley North, saying he had ineffectively tried every remedy.

"Pray, my lord", replied his friend, "did you ever try a clean shirt?"

For a long time the Duke had fancied marking the date, in 1783, when the Dukedom, created by Richard III, would have been in the Howard family for 300 centuries.

He had intended to invite all, both men and women, who had

descended from 'Jockey of Norfolk', the first duke who had been killed in battle at Bosworth Field.

"But having already," said he, "discovered six thousand persons sprung from him, a great number of whom are in very obscure and indigent circumstances, and believing, as I do, that as many more are in existence, I have abandoned the design!"

Cumbrian bard Robert Anderson summed him up in glorious style:
"First Graystok we'll nwotish,
The seat girt Norfolk,
A neame still to freemen and Englishmen dear.
You Cumbrian fwok may your sons and your grandsons,
Sec a rare statesman ever revere".

Thomas Bouch

THOMAS BOUCH

The Civil Engineer from Thursby

Outside the gale-force wind keened through the steel lattice work of the bridge standing just a few yards from the station, howling in concord with the frenzied dance of the dark waters whipped up below.

Inside the railway carriage Annie Cruickshank, thankful for her warm merino dress, pulled her buttoned jacket close, thrust her hands deep into her muff, and peered out through the window. St Fort station was all hustle and bustle on that Sunday evening, passengers were still boarding and the 4.15 p.m. train from Edinburgh, due in Dundee at 7.30pm, was running five minutes late.

With Annie, a housemaid at number 5, Moray Place, Edinburgh - home of the widowed Elizabeth Baxter - was her cousin, Eliza Smart. On a cold December night it was comforting to think that Dundee, their destination, was only fifteen minutes away. With a sudden jolt the train pulled away. It was 7.20pm. Slowly it moved on to the bridge and, buffeted by the gale, started the twelve-minute crossing of the Firth of Forth. Only minutes later a terror-stricken Annie and Eliza were clutching each other, eyes wide open with a sudden fear as their third class carriage tilted crazily towards the girders outside. Then, over the scream of the wind, came the tortured shriek of metal scraping metal. On St Fort's station platform a group of onlookers stood aghast. As they watched the train careered off the central section of the bridge to plunge to the wild waters and quicksands below.

John Watts, a surface-man, had watched from the signal cabin on the south shore. He said: "I could see the lights behind the guard's van and watched them further and further into the gloom until, suddenly they began to fall, whilst at the same moment bright flashes of light came from the spot where the front of the train would have been.

49

The derelict Tay Bridge after the disaster.

"I saw the lights disappear into the waves and the horrible truth became clear."

Another witness told how he had seen the lights of the train enter the bridge at the south end and had followed them across the lower span and into the high girders. "Then came a gust of wind more violent than any that preceded it. We then saw a sudden shower of fire, then the fire, with the lights of the train, seemed to descend to the river.

"Then there was nothing but darkness, broken only by the fitful appearance of a bright moon through an interstice of the black and rolling clouds."

Station officials rushed onto the bridge, crawling on their hands and knees to eventually reach a huge gap in the structure. All they could see in the moonlight were the stumps of the support piers with the water dashing over them.

Next day, in the dawn light of Monday, it could be seen that the thirteen great girders that spanned the navigable channel of the Tay had disappeared. Washed ashore was the flotsam that was a tragic reminder of the terrible disaster; three or four miles past Broughty Ferry were sleepers, carriage doors, the cushioned backs of First Class carriages. Here lay a

Seventy-five perished. there were no survivors.

workman's cap, there a black portmanteau with the initials A.S. A broken parcel of Christmas presents made a poignant sight, as did a lady's black straw hat trimmed with mauve velvet and black silk.

There were no survivors, all seventy five passengers perished and many bodies were washed out to sea. The first to be recovered was that of the housemaid Annie Cruikshank.

It was 1879. It was the biggest ever railway engineering disaster and it brought to a tragic end the brilliant career of Thomas Bouch, born in the Ship Inn at Thursby, son of a sea captain who had retired to live in Cumberland.

At school in Carlisle Thomas had been a bright pupil of Mr Joseph Hannah. Later, from 1839 until 1844, he had been apprenticed to the firm of Locke and Errington, who at that time were constructing the Carlisle and Lancaster Railway.

Debris of tragedy: the sad remnains of Bouch's Bridge over the Tay

Thomas later designed the Cockermouth, Keswick, Penrith and Eden Valley railway lines, was to become resident engineer on the famous Stockton and Darlington Railway, and, subsequently, Manager and Engineer of the Edinburgh and Northern Railway. Thomas Bouch was covered in glory when, in 1850, he created the first-ever railway ferry.

It was the inconvenience of the break in railway traffic caused by the estuaries of the Forth and Tay that led to his creating the 'floating railway'. March 7, 1850, was a gala day on Scotland's Firth of Forth, marking the launch of Bouch's revolutionary ferry on the line that linked Edinburgh, Perth, and Dundee.

Onlookers cheered as the paddle steamer Leviathan, only half-loaded for the special occasion, moved majestically away from the jetty and Granton to head for Burntisland on the opposite shore.

Bouch's engineering talents were of the highest, he had designed nearly 300 miles of railway in the north of England and Scotland and had also laid lines in London, Edinburgh, Glasgow and Dundee.

When, eventually, taking the railway across the River Tay by bridge was first thought of nothing was more natural than making Bouch the man for the job. He was renowned as a designer of bridges, and the splendid Redheugh Viaduct at Newcastle was a testimonial to his skills.

The bridge across the Forth, a series of lattice girders supported by more than fifty piers across the two-mile wide estuary, had opened on May 31, 1878. The first stone had been laid on the Fifeshire side on July 7, 1871. Construction had required 3,520 tons of cast iron, 90,600 feet of timber and 4,350,000 bricks.

Honours came the designer's way. Bouch was made a Freeman of Dundee. Queen Victoria and later the Prince of Wales crossed over the bridge. The Queen was not displeased, the following year Bouch was knighted. Great honours for a man born in a small Cumbrian village. But it was just one year later that the Tay bridge collapsed. A report spelled out just what had happened: "The columns must have been subjected to a terrible wrench, both are very much shattered. The south side outmost pier has one of its sides cleanly torn out... nothing remains intact of the ironwork, it has simply been smashed to pieces." Bouch was to be crucified. Said the Carlisle Patriot of July 9, 1880: "Our townsman Sir Thomas Bouch gets a terribly severe handling in the report of the enquiry into the fall of the Tay bridge. Never, probably, was there a more emphatic condemnation of a great work of engineering."

Two months previously Sir Thomas had given evidence to the inquiry, explaining his design but confessing he had made no provision for wind pressure. The court eventually decided: "The bridge was badly designed, badly constructed, and badly maintained, and its downfall was due to inherent defects in the structure which, sooner or later, must have brought it down. For the faulty design Sir Thomas is wholly responsible, and he is principally to blame for the defective construction."

A year later, at the age of 56, the disgraced Sir Thomas was dead. He had been living at 6, Oxford Terrace in Edinburgh, and died whilst visiting Moffat. He was buried in Edinburgh's Dean Cemetery, the pall bearers included his son William, and Joseph Hannah from Carlisle. His obituary said that the disaster had preyed heavily on his mind and had affected his health. After a lifetime of achievement his memorial sadly was to be that of disaster and death.

JANET WOODROW

The President's Mother from Carlisle

It was the year of 1835, and the packet ship that left the English port of Liverpool on November 10, carrying the emigrants seeking a new life in the United States of America, was ploughing its way across the Atlantic. Overhead the sails filled and cracked as the blustery winds carried her along. Standing on deck a young girl clung to a loose rope dangling from the main arm as she watched, fascinated by the waves and the movement of the vessel. It was then that a sudden squall hit the ship and she was swung out over the water, hanging dangerously over the seething ocean.

The short time she hung there seemed a lifetime to those watching from the ship, but then the vessel righted herself and nine year old Janet Woodrow was pulled to safety.

In many ways it was just as well, for with no Janet Long Beach would have had no Woodrow Wilson School, America would not have had a President Wilson, and Europe, battered by World War 1, would not have had a doughty fighter for the League of Nations.

Little Janet, born on December 26, 1826, emigrating to the USA with her preacher father, the Reverend Thomas Woodrow, her mother Marion and six other children, was later to become the mother of Woodrow Wilson, President of the United States from 1913 to 1921.

It was never to be an easy voyage. Thomas Woodrow was later to recall: "During the latter part of our long and perilous voyage of 62 days we were out of many things, and had been nearly seven weeks with an allowance of water, part of the time two quarts a day, and later on only one. "We had many fine days, but generally speaking we had gales in succession and violent head winds. We certainly at one time had little hope of seeing land. During most of the voyage my dear partner was sick and lay in bed. "We

Woodrow Wilson's mother and father.

Woodrow Wilson in the entrance lobby of the Crown and Mitre in 1908

often gave one another and our dear children and sister to the lord, expecting a watery grave.

"One dreadful night especially,I will never forget: a mighty sea broke over us, carried off our hatch and poured down on us in torrents.

"It struck the captain, who was halfway up the mizzenmast, carried off the galley and four sailors in it, but was providentially stopped by bulwarks.

"Very providentially it was not followed by another until our hatch was put up and lashed.

"Another evening when the ship was in full sail she was struck by a gale which tore most of our sails to rags. "I would never advise anyone to cross the Atlantic in Winter."

His "dear partner", Marion, died on February 16, just a month after surviving the perilous voyage .

The Reverend Thomas died at Columbus on April 27, 1877, his

Woodrow Wilson about to board the train at Carlisle Railway Station..

daughter Janet, known to the family as Jessie, married Joseph Ruggles Wilson, whose parents James, a printer, and Anne Adams both came from County Down in Ireland. Joseph was also a preacher, becoming Moderator of the Southern Presbyterian General Assembly in 1879, and dying at Princeton in 1903 at the time when his son Woodrow was President of the renowned university

In later years President Wilson was to travel to the English city of Carlisle, visiting the birthplace of his mother and the site of his grandfather's church.

Grandfather, the Rev Thomas Woodrow, had arrived from Paisley, in Scotland, in 1820 to become Minister of the Annetwell Street Congregational Chapel, living in the next-door manse.

In 1832 the family moved to Cavendish House, in one of the city's main streets, three years later they emigrated.

The Reverend's last service in the Annetwell Street chapel was on the Sunday before June 27, 1835. He took as his text the words from II Corinthians, Chapter i, verse 12: "Finally Brethren, farewell".

Wilson paid his first visit in 1896, cycling into the city on June 22. He stayed at the Central Hotel but could not find his mother's birthplace.

He returned in July, 1908, staying at the city's Crown and Mitre Hotel, this time discovering where his mother was born - "under the Castle Walls".

The city paid tribute to Woodrow Wilson on his third and final trip in 1918, en route for the World War I Peace Conference in Paris.

Wilson described his visit as a "Pilgrimage of the Heart when he arrived on December 29.

He was shown the site of his mother's birth, visited his grandfather's church, and addressed the congregation at the Lowther Street Congregational Church, the successor to the old chapel.

The finest honour bestowed on this grandson of a Carlisle preacher was initiated by the The Mayor of Carlisle, who proposed that the Honorary Freedom of the City be conferred on Woodrow Wilson, PhD., Litt.D., L.D., President of the United States "in recognition of his high qualities of statesmanship and the valuable services rendered by him as the head of the American Republic in connection with the Great War, in assisting the Allies to secure a lasting peace, freedom for the peoples of the world and the upholding of the rights of smaller nations in the contest waged by the Central Powers - Germany, Austria, Turkey and Bulgaria - for world domination."

MARTIN TALLENTS

Carer for Robert Graves from Hutton End

Eighty-three years ago the great guns on the Western Front fell silent. The Armistice of 1918 brought to an end four years of mindless warfare and the young men of Britain could return home.

But there were many who would never return, falling in their hundreds of thousands on the bloody battlefields of France. Some died a death that to this day brings shame to grieving families. They were shot at dawn by British firing squads after travesties of field courts martial had found shattered and shell-shocked men guilty of cowardice or desertion. MARTIN TALLENTS, a man now living in a quiet corner of Cumbria, has been witness to many such tales of World War I horror ...

If there had been birds in the trees they would have scattered, squawking, as the volley of shots shattered the dawn peace of the French farmyard.

But there were no birds. And the trees were grotesque parodies of nature, limbs blackened and twisted, standing stark against the early morning sky.

For this was war. Other blackened and twisted limbs, this time those of young men, lay scattered across a countryside rutted with ooze-filled trenches, where the death stench hung over the soldiers of World War I. As the dead-eyed firing squad splashed muddily away an officer stepped over the khaki-clad body slumped at the foot of a post, placed his pistol to its head and fired one more shot.

The young victim, barely eighteen, had been court-martialled and declared a coward.

Years later much wiser men were to recognise shell-shock and post

At home in Hutton End: Martin Tallents with Graves's book 'The White Goddess'.

trauma syndrome.

After days of non-stop cannon fire, after going "over the top" to advance towards the German lines - somehow surviving the swathes of lead spewed from machine guns traversing left to right then back again - and after days of listening to the nightmare screams of of dying men, guts hung out to dry on washing lines of barbed wire, this boy's brain could take no more. He had collapsed, a gibbering wreck of a human being...

One who did survive to tell the tales of horror was to become a close friend of Martin Tallents, who lives in Hutton-in-the-Forest, the small Cumbrian village near Penrith.

Born in 1921, he was the younger son of Sir Stephen Tallents, KCMG., CB., CBE., and Lady Bridget. The family home was St John's Jerusalem, a one-time Commandery of the Knights Hospitallers, set in Sutton-at-Hone, near Dartford in Kent.

Cressida Pemberton-Piggot

Seventy-five perished, there were no survivors.

Martin's niece, Cressida Pemberton-Piggott, a well-known London photographer - now Lady Inglewood - lives just around the corner at Hutton Hall, ancestral home of the Vane family.

But for 25 years Martin lived in the Majorcan village of Deya, where his best-loved friend was Robert Graves, the World War I officer, author and poet, whose autobiography - "Goodbye To All That" - is considered to be one of the most notable books of The Great War.

Martin's mother was a friend of Graves's daughter Catherine, and

61

when Lady Bridget died it was Catherine who suggested that Deya was the ideal place where he might recuperate after the funeral and the trauma of writing some 140 letters to those who had sent condolences.

Martin knew of Deya. He had once spent a fortnight's holiday in the village, during which he had visited a pension run by Graves' eldest son William and had been invited to stay for dinner. The two other guests were Robert and his wife Beryl. It was no surprise that when, in 1969, Martin arrived on the island for the second time Robert Graves helped to find him a house.

It was where Martin was to spend the next twenty-five years during which the war-shattered poet found in him a friend and confidante.

Says Martin: "Between 1969 and 1978 I organised daily tea parties. Anybody could come. Sometimes there were so many that they had to sit on the stairs in threes and fours. Sometimes there were two sessions - one at 4pm, another at 5pm. In that nine-year period some 3,000 sat down to tea!" Robert Graves, with Beryl, came every day. Later he was to tell Martin: "I don't know quite what I would have done if I hadn't had you to come to!"

Explains Martin: "It was where he could express his views but without anything going outside the house."

"Sometimes he wanted to keep his own counsel, and sometimes he wanted to talk. He might have been in the middle of a poem - often he rewrote his poems. Sometimes there were over thirty drafts.

"I think that sometimes he wanted to express his worries about all kinds of things.

"On some occasions it would take quite a time cheering him up. Usually it was when he was working on something.

"Once he said to me "Poetry is the truth, the truth suddenly strikes. It may go away for sometime, but it suddenly returns".

Another time he said: "What I would most like to do is write a poem; but cannot do that on purpose, or by accident". Says Martin modestly: "I was no expert on his work, but I could help him in many small ways and be a companionable kind of person for him".

In 1979 Robert Graves was diagnosed as suffering from Expressive Aphasia.

"After 1978, when he started to stay at his home, Casa Salerosa, and no longer came to tea, I used to go and shave him, and lift him, to help the nurses, a dedicated team working under the village doctor, Javier Peri.

"Sometimes in the mornings, and every evening, I would help lift Robert from bed to chair, to dining room, to fireside and then back again".

Martin, to this day, recalls the death of Robert Graves. "William, his oil geologist son, who worked all over the world, should have been back three weeks earlier. He waited those three weeks. When, at last, he entered the room, he opened one eye, looked at William, then passed away".

In his book "Goodbye To All That", Graves had told how he had been appointed a member of a Field General Court Martial that was to decide the fate of a sergeant charged with shamefully casting away his arms in the presence of the enemy. The man, maddened by an intense bombardment, had thrown away his rifle and run with the rest of his platoon. A secret and confidential army order had laid down that in the case of men tried for their life on other charges, sentence might be mitigated if conduct in the field had been exemplary. Cowardice, however, was punishable only by death, and no medical excuses could be accepted. Graves, as a Captain, had no choice between sentencing the man to death and refusing to take part in the proceedings. He said: "If I refused, I should be court-martialled myself, and a reconstituted court would sentence the sergeant to death anyhow. Yet I could not sign a death verdict for an offence which I might myself have committed in similar circumstances".

He avoided the dilemma by finding another captain qualified and willing to take his place.

Graves also confirmed that such executions were frequent in France, telling how, when he arrived at Le Havre in May, 1915, he had read the back files of army orders at the rest camp.They contained some twenty reports of men shot for cowardice or desertion.

A few days later a minister in the House of Commons, answering a question from a pacifist member, denied that any sentence of death for a military offence had been carried out in France on any member of His Majesty's forces. There were many other tales of the war years that Graves confided to Martin Tallents, who recalls an incident that showed that the war poet - who spent more years on active service than almost any other - years later still suffered from the horror of the trenches.

He tells how Robert was walking with a young friend towards the village of Deya during the Fiesta of St John the Baptist when a rocket soared skywards, marking the start of an event.

Robert started to run forward,

"Stop, Robert, stop," called his companion.

"If you try to stop me I'll knock you down," was the retort. Says Martin: "His mind had gone back sixty years and he thought it was a Very light signalling an attack". Another time, as Graves was taking tea at Martin's home, a boy handed him a poem and asked if he would read it. He did so, but then told the youngster: "Well, it's alright - but perhaps you haven't died enough times yet!"

Martin himself is no stranger to war.

He graduated from Cambridge in 1942 with a BA in architecture. Vacations found him on London's Euston Station helping to cook 700 meals a night for soldiers in transit; the next night the same task would await him at King's Cross; the night after he would be driving a mobile canteen from Gatti's, in The Strand, taking meals to firemen fighting the flames of the Blitz.

He also saw his share of blood and guts, serving five years at sea in the Royal Navy.

He had first joined the Royal Naval Volunteer Reserve as an Ordinary Seaman, and in 1942 was serving in the light cruiser Cleopatra, escorting convoys to Malta, when a 6-inch shell from an enemy cruiser struck the after starboard side of the bridge, wrecking the air defence position, killing one officer and fourteen men. Another officer and four men were wounded.

Martin was one of the ship's company detailed to clear bodies from the wreckage and was Mentioned in Despatches for distinguished service.

Thirty years later he recalled the incident, writing a poem - "Shellburst" - now in the Imperial war Museum in London, the first stanza of which reads:

> *Have you ever put men in weighted sacks,*
> *In a rising storm off Malta?*
> *In the slop of their blood and the smell of cordite,*
> *When something's happened that you can't alter.*
> *Up on the bridge, in front of the stacks,*
> *Wearing best woollen gloves*

For they're long past a handshake
Bound for the water in canvas sacks,
Each to be sunk with torpedo weight.
For the light has has gone out of some sailors you knew
In the flash of a shell that was all too true.

Martin went on to serve in the mine-sweeping trawler HMS Willow and Motor Minesweeper 290.

He rose from the lower deck to the rank of lieutenant, and during the 1944 D-day landings was serving in HMS Lennox, an Algerine class fleet sweeper operating off Gold Beach. Before his move to Majorca peacetime had found him a job equally as delicate as mine-sweeping, assisting Professor Hans Beren who was restoring the Queen's Buckingham Palace porcelain collection. He spent another eighteen years intermittently restoring the Church of St John the Baptist at Sutton-on-Hove, which had been bomb damaged, designing and making new prayer desks and chairs for the sanctuary. Today Martin, who, in his secluded Cumbrian cottage, will serve you tea - delicate sandwiches and the jam served up in the beaten silver bowl that was a gift from Robert Graves - is a rare living link with just one officer who suffered so much that he often hallucinated, seeing dead bodies as he walked the streets of London. Despite modern-day attitudes that can understand the psychological effect of continuous bombardment and trench warfare the British Government, to this day, continues to turn down requests that the sad young men shot at dawn should receive a posthiumous pardon. Too big a task after so many years is the official reason.

However, representatives of half a dozen families have been allowed to lay a wreath at the Cenotaph paying tribute to the 306 known to have been executed.

But for many families the shame that should not be lives on. Perhaps it should be left to Martin Tallent's friend Robert Graves and the other war poets to remember them kindly. In Graves' poem "Recalling War" one stanza reads:

And we recall the merry way of guns,
Nibbling the walls of factory or church,
Like a child, piecrust; felling groves of trees,
Like a child, dandelions with a switch,

> *Machine guns rattle toy-like from a hill,*
> *Down in a row the brave tin soldiers fall:*
> *A sight to be recalled in elder days,*
> *When learnedly the future we devote*
> *To yet more boastful visions of despair.*

Siegried Sassoon, possibly the most gifted of the War poets - certainly the most cynical - was a lifelong friend of Graves. He wrote:

> *I knew a simple soldier boy,*
> *Who grinned at life in simple joy,*
> *Slept soundly through the lonesome dark,*
> *And whistled early with the lark.*
>
> *In Winter trenches, cowed and glum,*
> *With crumps and lice and lack of rum,*
> *He put a bullet through his brain,*
> *No-one spoke of him again.*
> *You smug-faced crowds with kindling eye,*
> *Who cheer when soldier lads march by,*
> *Sneak home and pray you'll never know*
> *The hell where youth and laughter go.*

Modern-day poet Paul Birtill was more succint in his "The Secret Crier". It read:

> *The old man wept privately making sure the windows were closed and mortise lock was on the front door.*
>
> *He had been caught crying once before in the trenches on the Somme and had been threatenedwith a .38 revolver ...*

Robert Graves visited Cumberland in 1927, two years before moving to Majorca. He was visiting his first wife, Nancy, who, suffering from bad nerves, had left their home in Islip to stay with her brother Ben. She worked on a farm and lived in a cottage near Walton.

Brother Ben was the artist Ben Nicholson, whose first marriage was to Winifred, daughter of Lady Cecilia Howard, grandaughter of the Earl of Carlisle. Winifred was to become a well-known artist in her own right.

HENRY SCOTT SAWYER

Chemist's Son and Malayan Adventurer from Carlisle

Henry Scott Sawyer must have inherited his great-grandfather's sense of adventure; for whilst his father and grandfather were content to run the family pharmacy business on the corner of Carlisle's Fisher Street, the young Henry found work in more exotic lands. Grandad James had done his share of soldiering, in 1813 taking part in the battle of Busaco - fought during the Peninsular war - in which, on September 7, 1810, the British Infantry put the French to flight. He ended his Royal Horse Artillery days by surviving the battle of Waterloo.

The veteran of many wars retired to become Mine Host of the Kings Head in Fisher Street, where, with his wife Elizabeth, he settled to bring up a son and four daughters. In 1854 the old soldier retired from the city centre inn and, with wife and daughters, left Carlisle. Son James, then 37 years old, who had opened a chemist's shop, remained in the city.

He, in turn, had three sons, one of whom, Henry, born in 1852, took over the pharmacy when his father died in 1875. He had married a farmer's daughter, born at Hilltop Farm, Westcott, near Dorking in Surrey, and was content to be a successful businessman and a well-known breeder of show-ring bulldogs. He made a name for himself by carrying on a war of words in "The Dog World" magazine over the efficacy of brewer's yeast in the treatment of distemper in dogs!

But if Henry opted to stay at home it was his son, Henry Scott Sawyer, who answered the call of adventure and later emigrated to the other side of the world; he had an insatiable wanderlust and on January 15, 1911, penned these words:

Soon I will leave the fairy scenes,
My childhood's love, my home;

Leave parents, friends, and kindred few,
Across the sea to roam.
The rocky headlands, as I sail,
Fade slowly on the sea,
I go to seek the stranger's fate,
So bid adieu to thee."

Carlisle couple Brian and Eileen Henderson accidentally shed some light on Henry's adventures. Whilst attending the funeral of Lawrence Howe - a one-time sub-editor with the Carlisle Journal who left to join the Nottingham Post in 1946 and settled there with his wife Sylvia, nee Garnett - they noticed a box in the garage of his house in Nottingham. It contained papers, drawings and photographs that, over the years, had been sent to England by Henry to an Aunt Lucy, who could have been one of his father's four sisters.

Henry junior had been sketching in France, one of his cartoons was signed St Claire.

In 1910 he was in Holland, a snapshot taken in 1910 showed canal-side houses. In January 1911 he was staying at the French Hotel De Ville in Arras. He then visited Belgium, photographing The Guildhall and The Exchange in Brussels.

In August 1920 he was suffering from nervous exhaustion, in a short note to Aunt Lucy (one of his father's four sisters, all born in Carlisle) writing:

"I thought you would like to have a copy of three of my sketches for this year.

Sorry I cannot write at length as I am again on sick leave and have been ordered to rest."

That year had found Henry in Sydney, Australia, working in the "Existing Lines Branch" of the New South Wales Government's Tramways and Railways. He was a talented cartoonist, and used his artistic talent in the cause of "safety-first", contributing cartoons to the company's monthly "Safety First" newsletter.

Henry Sawyer also had a curious sense of humour. On January 1, 1927 he penned these two odd stanzas, presumably after the death of a colleague:

*The death angel smote Alexander McGhee
And gave him protracted repose.
He wore a checked shirt and a number nine shoe,
And had a pink wart on his nose.*

*No doubt he is happier dwelling in space,
Over there on the evergreen shore.
So his friends are informed that the funeral takes place
Tomorrow, at a quarter past four.*

What then happened to Henry is not known. The latest date found in the small box of papers, drawings and photos discovered in Nottingham was 1927.

But more distant shores beckoned. Just one month later he was heading East on board the SS Borneo, calling in at Port Said to take on coal fuel and then passing through the Suez Canal.

A photograph dated April 1, 1911 shows privileged passengers on the promenade deck; one writes a letter, another snoozes in his deck chair, another reads. Leisure time for the gentry while below others work ship. Another of Henry's photos shows Lascars, the native lower deck workers, going ashore after "Sunday Parade."

He was out and about with his camera when the SS Borneo called in at Ceylon - now Sri Lanka - snapping a street scene complete with rickshaw cabbie and passenger. In Colombo he stayed at the Gold Face Hotel, an imposing building with top floor verandas looking out over the waving palm trees below.

Henry was heading East to work on the Nordaval rubber plantation in Malaya. the snapshots he sent home included those of a a male worker called "Fancy Pollie", and one of a water carrier, two cans slung from a bamboo pole resting on her shoulder. Timber chalets set in a clearing served as a hospital.

The steamship "Lady Weld" - named after lady Philomena, wife of Sir Frederick Weld, the British Government's man in charge of the Straits settlements of Penang, Malacca, Singapore and Labuan - brought up provisions from Singapore.

Henry really lived the life of Riley. Another picture showed him seated outside his house wearing jodhpurs, knee-length woollen socks and highly polished shoes. He is seated at an ornate cane wickerwork table on which his drink stands. Standing respectfully behind him was his white-suited houseboy.

His idyllic way of life was not to last. The First World War found him back in Britain in 1915. A card sent home from the Royal Navy's base in Devonport and marked "On Active Service" was sent to his mother, living at 12, Howard Place. It showed a ship, the SS Orsova and was captioned "Off to the war, May, 1915." The message read:

"This is the boat we are on. Can you send one dozen safety razor blades like dad's to the above address as I had no time to get anything. Am VERY well, Love H."

He was obviously a medic and at sea. The address was No 4124, 28th Sanitary Section, RAMC, c/o GPO, Mediterranean.

Just five months later Henry Sawyer's war was over. A photograph taken in Malta shows him in hospital blues standing with six other patients and a Sister of the Queen Alexander's Royal Naval Nursing Service.

Another card, this time showing the SS Braemar castle, was captioned "Invalided home, October 27, 1915."

In 1916 he was recuperating by the seaside from where he sent his mother a sketch of a bathing belle relaxing in a deckchair, in the background a line of bathing machines. After the war the other side of the world was the next port of call for the itchy-footed Henry. By 1919 he was in Australia. He created his own New Year greeting card which he sent to his Aunt Lucy, a pen and ink drawing of a breeze-blown young lady in the height of twenties fashion standing by the seashore. His caption came from the heart, showing a nostalgia for his old life but hope for the future. It read:

There is a past which is gone for ever;
but there is a future which is still our own.

WILLIAM GEORGE ARMSTRONG

The Mayor of Newcastle frm Wreay

The diary of southern planter Edmund Ruffin:
1861: "Before 4am the drums beat for parade and our company was speedily on the march to the batteries to which they were to man. At 4.30 a signal shell was thrown from a mortar battery at Fort Johnson, which had been before ordered to be taken as the command for immediate attack - and the firing from all the batteries bearing on Fort Sumpter began in the order arranged, which was that the discharges should be two minutes apart, and the round of all the pieces and batteries to be completed in 32 minutes and then to begin again..."

1865: The smoke of cannon fire swirled around the sweating grey-clad gunners. It was a simple ritual they followed; load, fire, reload, fire, reload. Shells screamed from the red hot barrels to slam into the enemy.

Sadly, facing the fire were their blue-uniformed fellow-countrymen, they, too, feeding their guns, returning salvo after salvo to slash through the ranks of the Confederate Army.

For this was civil war, ripping the heart out of the America of the 1860s.

Here was Gettysburg, defining battle of the conflict that for four years had tragically set neighbour against neighbour, fathers against sons. And back in Britain, far from the noise of battle, was a man, a son of a Cumbrian, who had invented, and whose company had manufactured, the new-fangled guns with the rifled barrels that made directing fire so much more accurate.

The irony was that it was a war in which William George Armstrong's company had nothing to lose; they had supplied both sides with their three-inch rifled guns, so superior to those produced in America.

The armaments supremo's father, another William, was a Cumbrian,

William George Armstrong - made a fortune from armaments

born in Wreay in 1777, and christened at St Mary's Church in Carlisle, the son of Bewcastle-born George Armstrong. His mother was Wigton girl Jane Wintrop, daughter of Robert Wintrop and christened in Wigton's St Mary's Church in February, 1741. George and Jane had married on June 15, 1768, and were living in Wreay after moving from Bewcastle.

Some 22 years later the young William had left the village to live in

Newcastle, where he prospered, establishing a thriving corn-merchant's business on the city's Quayside. He was a model citizen, a member of the city's Literary and Philosophical Society and a keen worker for charity: those who knew him said: "Every good project in the Tyneside city had a warm supporter in the Wreay yeoman's son." He took his civic duties seriously; in 1851 he became Mayor of Newcastle, he also became a magistrate, a River Commissioner and a Deputy Lieutenant

In November, 1810, his son was born, christened William George Armstrong, who, after an education at Bishop Auckland Gramrnar School, became articled to Samuel Donkin, a solicitor friend of his father, later becoming a partner in the practice. When not behind his lawyer's desk he indulged in his hobby - engineering. He had an inventive mind. In 1842 he constructed a hydro-electric generator, inspired by seeing an engine-man's accidental discharge of static electricity from a Northumberland colliery boiler.

It's possible he found the law, if not an ass, as dry as dust, for in 1844 he abandoned his practice. Engineering was his true forte and he wanted to spend more time in scientific experiments.

In 1846 his interest shifted to hydraulics, persuading wealthy Newcastle businessmen to back him. The result were his hydraulic cranes, powered with the help of the Whittle Dene Water Company, then, encouraged by his success, William Armstrong founded the Newcastle Cranage Company, based at Elswick. It was later to achieve a degree of lasting fame by its mention in the traditional Geordie song The Blaydon Races, in which it is described as "Armstrong's Factory."

Because his hydraulic machinery depended on water for power, in 1850 he invented a hydraulic accumulator - a large water-filled cylinder with a piston that could raise the water pressure in the cylinder and the supply pipes to 600 pounds a square inch, making possible the use of hoists, capstans, turntables and dock gates in any situation. Next he made improvements to the guns used by the British army, recommending the use of breech loading, rifled barrels and elongated shells. Armstrong's first gun appeared in 1855, the first modem cannon compared with those of the Middle Ages, and in 1859 the Elswick Ordnance Company was founded. Later he was to become Engineer of Rifled Ordnance at Woolwich Arsenal.

The Crimean War in 1850 created a demand for more modem armaments. The factory rose to the occasion, William's 18lb breech loading gun was just one of many Armstrong weapons recognised as the best in the world. Russia bought them, so did Japan, as well as the two armies fighting the American Civil war. This success make him an extremely wealthy man. From all sides honours showered upon him. At home, in 1843, he was elected a Fellow of the Royal Society. In 1887 he was created Baron Armstrong of Cragside. From overseas came more awards; he was made a Grand Officer of the Order of St Maurice and Lazarus of Italy; Knight Commander of the Dannebrog of Denmark, Knight Commander of Charles III of Spain, and Knight Commander of Francis Joseph of Austria. In 1863 he was President of the British Association, in 1882 President of the Institution of Civil Engineers, and was three times President of the Institution of Mechanical Engineers.

He was Sheriff of Northumberland in 1883.

As an immensely wealthy man - he owned Bamburgh Castle as well as 16,000 acres of land - he could afford to indulge in his passion for art. Only the best was good enough for him. On the walls of Cragside, his home near Rothbury, hung works by Millais, Turner, Rosetti and Constable. Gragside was the first home in the world to be lit by hydro-electric power. His London club was The Atheneum, and in the 1830s he had a third home built in Newcastle's Jesmond Dene, most of which he owned and where he took up landscape gardening. In 1833 he donated Jesmond Dene to the people of Newcastle.

In May, 1835, he had married Margaret, the daughter of William Ramshaw, of Bishop Auckland, but they had no children.

Two centuries before, his Armstrong ancestors had been feared throughout the Border country. They were raiders who looted and pillaged the countryside. William Armstrong, of Cumbrian stock, made his money the honest way, using his brain, not brawn.

When, on December 27, 1900, he died at Cragside he left a fortune of £ 1,399,000.

JOHN ROBERSTON SCOTT

The Countryman from Wigton

"On the space in front of the parish church the cattle, sheep and pigs were penned, pulled, and poked about and sold. The canny, well-fed, chattering farmers, some in local woollens, were accompanied by their shrewd, resourceful womenfolk, who brought with them baskets of butter and eggs and sometimes a few hens, and had their minds not only on what they had to sell but on what later they were, with due consideration, to buy.
These farm folk arrived in light carts or easy, decorous gigs with iron-rimmed wheels, clattering along streets paved with large cobbles from the river..."

It was market day in Wigton in the 1870s. Describing the scene years later was John William Robertson-Scott, born in April, 1866, the second of eight children of David Young Crozier Scott, commercial traveller and temperance orator, who with his wife Janet had moved to Wigton from Scotland just before John's birth.

The Cumbrian lad who had peered through the windows of his Georgian home to watch the market day scene recalled it graphically in a biography penned nearly eighty years later. As a writer he was well qualified. When just twenty-one years old he was working in Fleet Street as a freelance journalist, supporting his widowed mother, his brother and three sisters. His father, who he had once described as 'not only a teetotaller and non-smoker, but a believer in cold baths and a disbeliever in bottles of medicine', had died when he was only 43 years old. In 1887 he had joined the prestigious London paper The Pall Mall Gazette. When, in 1893, its editor, Sir Edward Cook, left to found The Westminster Gazette John Robertson-Scott went with him. Six years later he transferred to the Daily Chronicle but resigned the same year. The Chronicle supported the Boer War; Robertson-Scott could not! He then

John Roberson Scott at work.

decided to live and work in the country. His articles published in The Country Gentleman and The Field saw him developing an individual style in which he could tell townspeople about the lives of farmers and smallholders, farm-workers and landowners, how they lived and made a living but without confusing technicalities.

Robertson-Scott was over military age when was broke out in 1914. Two years later he was in Japan where he stayed six years, travelling 6,000 miles studying farming and rural life and it was there that he founded and edited a magazine called The New East. He returned to England to live in Ibury, a hamlet in Oxfordshire, and in 1927 found his ideal niche in the world of publishing. At the age of 61 he founded a quarterly magazine, The Countryman.

He and his wife Elspeth did everything. They were business and advertisement managers, editor and sub-editor as well as the principal contributors. Despite never having more than £500 capital they made it the

John Robertson Scott at home with his pets.

Caricature of Scott as a Japanese nurse-girl.

(Caricature of the Author as a Japanese Nurse Girl, by Elizabeth Keith)

most successful publishing venture of the time. In 1943 Robertson-Scott sold The Countryman but for four more years remained as editor. He had the magic touch. On the magazine's twentieth anniversary testimonials poured in by their hundreds. Politicians, poets, actors and actresses were among those who loved the magazine. Edith Evans, the actress later appointed Dame, wrote, as did famous author Kingsley Martin. Poet Walter De La Mare sent his congratulations, and another famous author, AA Milne, wrote: "My heartiest congratulations and best wishes. If only it were our own twentieth birthday we were celebrating! You have so identified yourself with the review that it is difficult to imagine one without the other. For this reason I shall wish you, rather than it, a long and prosperous maturity."

Later, in the 1950s, John Robertson-Scott wrote a series of autobiographical articles in which he vividly described the countryside and city of his young days. He had watched the coming of the first steam engines used in Cumberland for ploughing, recalling: "When they arrived at Aspatria Station the amazed crowd shouted "Yon'll nivver stur by thursels." But they did, and puffed in a stately way out of the station yard. The crowd said: "They'll nivver git up t'broo!' But they ascended the hill sturdily. Then the cry was 'They'll nivver ploo!' But they did plough to general satisfaction."

His parents eventually moved into Carlisle. Robertson-Scott recalled: "Next door to us lived a military man, in appearance and bearing of his era, who commanded at the Castle and had a fine Newfoundland dog. The dignified animal never quite understood that it had to walk behind, and not beside, its master. 'Four yards, sir - four yards I say!' the Colonel would call out as he stalked along the pavement, and the abashed animal would fall back from his master's side to his heels.

"With the Colonel's boys I frequented the castle. As we explored more of it than was ordinarily open to the public, the dank dungeons and the comfortless living places. I understood how Mary Queen of Scots and others before her had been used. I was saved from life from some illusions about castles, Plantagenets and the good old times." He vividly recalled his schooldays. He said: "Among my school fellows I was the leader of the Liberals and another boy the leader of the Conservatives. We wrote and circulated party periodicals, and we were the only boys of he hundred or more school who in afterlife went into journalism. My editorial rival succeeded to his father's local Conservative weekly, still edits it and has been President of the Newspaper Society and the Press Association..." That school fellow was John Burgess, later Sir John, whose sons today are still directors of Cumbria Newspapers, publishers of the Cumberland News and the Evening News & Star in Carlisle.

Others at the school included the Redmayne of Wigton tailoring fame, F N Hepworth, whose colour tin printing firm later became Metal Box, and John Haughan, one-time county architect for Cumberland.

The city he knew in his younger days was faithfully recorded. "Skiddaw was in view at Carlisle, as at the little market town of my birth. We also looked upon the fells at the end of Pennines and upon the Cheviots.

"It is no small blessing to have lived one's boyhood near fine hills and by the banks of a noble river and under the shadow of a castle which had its part in history.

"The Eden is memorable, whether in its grave amplitude as it flows through between Stanwix (of the Roman Wall) and the castle, or, romantically through a dell at Corby, where, for the first time in my life, I was in a boat; I can still hear the sound of the oars in the rowlock. I watched the salmon coming up from the sea - sometimes they suffered from a disease and rubbed themselves against stones in the banks - and got pleasure from the names of the tributaries, the Caldew - I thought it meant cauld (cold) dew - and the Petteril. "I was a young citizen of no mean city, for Carlisle goes back to the beginnings of English history. There - the first spot at which the Estuary of the Solway could be forded - ran the Roman Wall; there, at Stanwix, in the grounds of a subscriber toe The Countryman, are the remains of a fort larger than any other fort on the wall - it was equal to housing a cavalry regiment of a thousand men. A proud memory was that the city that grew up was strong enough to hold its own after the retirement of the Romans.

Robertson-Scott many matter-o-fact details: "Saturday the farmer's daughter came in the cart to collect the week's milk money, and no-one knew anything about bovine tuberculosis. There in the cart was a brass-bound barrel of such buttermilk as I have seldom tasted since - it had lumps of butter in it - a large closed pail of cream and a collection of shining measures from gill to quart."

This weekly ritual sowed the seeds for his later fascination in all things rural. He wrote: "To the whitewashed farmhouse at Newby which sent us this good food I went to sometimes in the holidays. I appreciated the kindness of our Scottish hosts and the way they fed me and their farmhands - we all ate at the same table.

"I saw, at one time or another, ploughing, harrowing and rolling, milking and mowing, haycocking and corn harvesting, the shining and winnowing, potato growing, root-cutting, cow and pig feeding, nudden-making and the care taken of the implements taken by the farmer's sons..

"In the fields I heard the calls of the Whaup (Curlew) and the clamorous craiks (corncrakes) at close o' day. Do not think that I looked rapturously upon a countryside with no failings. I saw drunkenness and some superstition, was old enough to know of illegitimacy, and was curious to notice that, as far as I could see, the fatherless children were just the same,

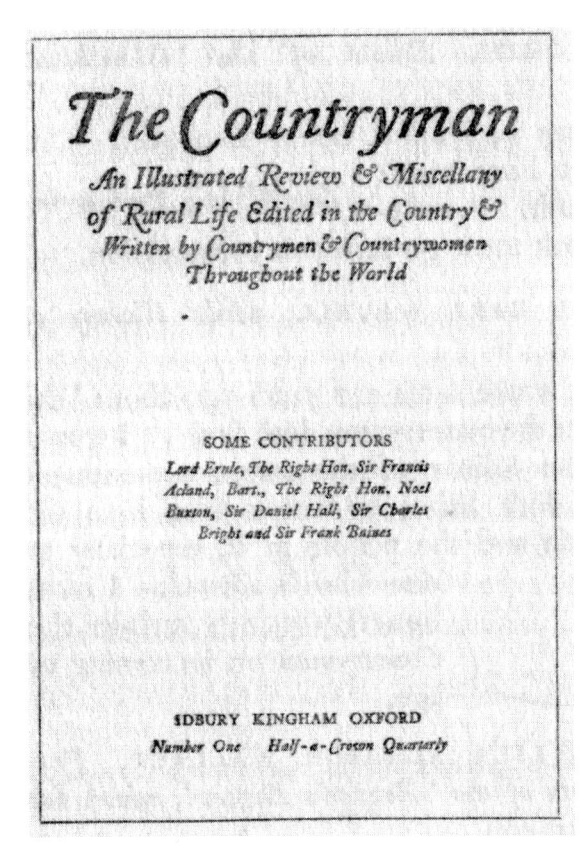

The first copy of The Countryman.

sometimes kinder, it seemed, than legitimates, and were just as good-looking"

Meanwhile, in the nearby city, times were changing. It was there that he witnessed the advent of the hard-tyred penny-farthing bicycle. He recalled: "The rider of which wore a blue serge jacket, and knickers, and a pork-pie hat, and mounted from a box or stone, or, more gallantly, from the pedal of the big wheel or a little iron step in the frame. In going downhill, if he were adventurous - the free-wheel had not been invented - he flung his legs over the bars, and sometimes, if, for instance, the wheel bumped against a stone, came down with a nasty crack on his head, not to mention some broken spokes."

When John Robertson-Scott retired in 1947 he was made a Companion of Honour. Two years later Oxford made him an honorary MA. But perhaps the finest testimonial to the lad born in Cumberland came from the Poet Laureate. John Masefield, on The Countryman's twenty-first, wrote "Let me wish The Countryman a happy birthday and many prosperous returns. It has never failed, in any number since it began, to interest, to cheer, and to delight its readers. It had most deservedly prospered. No magazine of the last generation has kept a finer standard, has printed more wonderful illustrations, or preserved more of what is precious in the country life of yesterday and today.

"This has been done superbly; but with this, there has ever been a most hopeful insistence on all fine and forward standards, in farming, the basis or right life anywhere, and in the humane arts, the fruits of all right life."

John Robertson-Scott died in 1962.

ARTHUR C ASTOR

The Man of the Theatre from Silloth

The trio's music was in the style of Stefan Grapelli's 'Hot Club de France'. Their costumes and make-up, to say the least, were odd.

Their humour was crazy, but it appealed to the audience of war-weary troops packing out the Bellini Theatre in Naples for a Festival of Entertainment, including a talent competition, organized by the Central Pool of Artists, the wartime entertainment unit that used servicemen to produce morale-boosting shows.

The comedy and music of the Bill Hall trio took the place by storm! They were not actually competing: they were part of the bill that provided a framework for the contest, and were sandwiched between the Polish Ballet Company and top-of-the-bill singing star Gracie Fields.

But, more importantly, they caught the eye of one of the talent show judges who must have been the first professional to spot the trio's star quality, and, in particular, that of the guitarist.

The judge was Arthur C Astor, the international showbiz giant most improbably from Silloth, Cumberland's small seaside town.

The guitar-playing comedian was Spike Milligan, in later years one of the legendary Goons.

In his book "Where Have All The Bullets Gone?" Spike recalled: "During our act we have been spotted by an impresario in the Judges' Box who sends us a note promising untold riches in the future".

Astor's quickly pencilled note read:
"Will book your act as seen tonight if you want to play Variety. Let me know
1/ Men likely to be available
2/ Where to find you

My card is attached."

It was signed AC Astor, the name by which the pre-war world of variety knew him, and as such, the name under which, in 1936, he had purchased Carlisle's Her Majesty's Theatre.

AC Astor had every right to be in that judges' box - he was no stranger to the world of variety that had its heyday between the two world wars. He was a top ventriloquist; his puppet a face painted on his hand, the index finger and thumb forming the mouth.

Before the Second World War he had toured America and Canada several times, and it was during those early days that he had made three short films. In 1928 he had appeared in one made by a company called Phonofilm, and was titled "AC Astor with Sentimental Mac". In 1932 Pathtone had him featured in "Wedding Bells Are Ringing For Sally", and in 1936 Pathe Pictorial (NS 20) he appeared in "Spike Sullivan's Girl".

As well as the USA and Canada he toured Australia. He was a favourite of King George V, being more than once invited to give a private royal performance at Windsor Castle, and was chosen to appear in several Royal Command Performances.

But in 1892 AC Astor had come into the world as plain Thomas Ferguson, son of William Ferguson, a water engineer who owned his own plumbing business, and his second wife Jane, living in Silloth's Esk Street.

As a teenager he was soon bitten by the showbiz bug. He formed a small band of pierrots that entertained seaside crowds on the green between the main street the waters of the Solway, and it was there that he developed the art of ventriloquism that was to lead to theatrical fame.

By rights Arthur Ferguson - for some reason he was known as Astor by his family - should have been a chemist and was once apprenticed to John Hunter, who had his pharmacy in Carlisle's Bank Street. But stage-struck Arthur decided that pills and potions were not his medicine. Hearing of a band of variety actors travelling from town to town he packed a bag and ran off to join them, taking with him his ventriloquist act from his Silloth green days.

Family legend has it that it broke his mother's heart. The Carlisle Patriot of March 23, 1906, reported the inquest into her death - she was found hanging in the kitchen. Her GP, a Dr Crerar, gave evidence that she had been latterly rather despondent.

However, showbiz did not at first lift the curtain on fame and fortune for young Arthur, the small company struggled, often finding themselves in remote towns with little or no cash.

Donald Peers, a top of the bill crooner in the 'forties and 'fifties, had a tale to tell of AC's early, impoverished days.

Peers had an Uncle Elwyn who ran the Coliseum, a small cinema with a stage set in the small South Wales town of Ystalyfera, which was built over the newspaper office and printing works ran by two other uncles. Elwyn booked the "forthcoming attractions" and was the family showman. .

Whatever the limitations of the Coliseum may have been, many artists appeared on its tiny stage and had cause to be thankful for a week's engagement there. From time to time even small theatrical companies would find their way to Ystalyfera.

Said Peers: "In 1949, when I was singing in Blackpool, A. C. Astor, that accomplished ventriloquist, told me how he had "played" Ystalyfera. He had already described the experience in one of his most readable and entertaining articles in The Stage.

With a company of other young performers he had been touring South Wales. Small profits turned to losses, and eventually they were stranded.

The owner of the Coliseum, Ystalyfera, hearing of their sad story, agreed to help them out. He offered them the use of the theatre so that they might at least raise the fare back to London.

"I shall never forget it," Arthur Astor told Donald Peers. "Not because there were no dressing-rooms - heaven knows, we were used to going without that luxury - but it was the first and only time that I had to change and make up in a newspaper office. We rigged up screens and, as we put on our costumes, dodged in and out among the printing presses!" AC never forgot the days of eking out a living and was always ready to help out an actor or company going through a bad time.

As a young man he had married an actress, Ivy (?) by whom he had two children. The son, Arthur, became an accountant in Canada, their daughter, Kathleen - known always to AC as "Girlie" - kept up the theatrical tradition by marrying the famous Laurie Lupino Lane. Laurie's father, Lupino

Lane, was born in the same year as AC Astor and later they became firm friends. Carlisle man Frank Graham, as a schoolboy, earned pocket money at Her Majesty's Theatre as the call-boy whose duty it was to knock on dressing room doors to warn artistes they were on stage soon. He has vivid memories of AC. "He always smoked cheroots - you could smell him before you saw him." Frank recalled one of his last visits. "He came to see the pantomime Robinson Crusoe. Her Majesty's had challenged stage history and had a male Principal Boy. Danny Purches, the 'Gypsy Singer', played the part instead of the traditional leggy lady.

In 1936 AC took some time out, his thoughts turning to Cumberland and home. It was the year he bought Her Majesty's Theatre in Carlisle's Lowther Street and proceeded to put the city on the entertainment map.

At the same time he also bought Howe End Farm at Thursby, as well as a small town house in Chapel Street, just round the corner from the theatre.

Manager of Her Majesty's and a great friend of AC - a friendship that - was John Sullivan, an ideal man for the job; he had a love for showbiz and produced many a Gangshow which saw stage spectaculars featuring the Scout troops of Carlisle and the county as well as the occasional surprise appearance of John marching out from the wings beating a huge bass drum perched on his rather generous tummy, other local talent was polished to perform in the regular Pick Of The Town shows. He was not averse to a touch of melodrama in himself; these shows required Sunday afternoon dress rehearsals, at the end of which John would collapse into a seat, mop his brow and wearily say to Stan Vassey - assistant manager and one-time adagio dancer - "Take me home Stan"!

Home was in the country where John's wife Belle lived and where he sometimes hosted an end of show party; a delightful redheaded niece served drinks. She had an amazing memory, after one visit each guest's particular favourite was always remembered.

In 1939 AC divorced Ivy, to wed again in the 'forties. This time his bride was glamorous singer Phyllis Robbins.

AC knew all the top people of the showbiz world - their names could have filled a bill that no amount of money could buy: Noel Coward, Sophie Tucker, Tessie O'Shea, The Crazy Gang, Rene Houston and Jack Hylton. Hundreds of others included his old friend the great Lupino Lane. Lupino

Lane, born Henry George Lupino, was only four years old when he made his first stage appearance - a walk-on part in a benefit performance for the famous Vesta Tilley. It was Lupino Lane, in the musical Me And My Girl who made famous the Londoners' dance The Lambeth Walk. His son Laurie went into films and married AC's daughter Kathleen.

The showbiz bug was ever with him and he was always ready to help out an amateur company and made personal appearances at charity shows in Carlisle. I can recall one wonderful night in the `sixties when, at Her Majesty's during a "Pick of The Town" show featuring local artistes, AC, unannounced, walked out from the wings with the cute little puppet and enthralled an audience with his act. If paid for it would have cost a bomb = in January 1921 AC was appearing at the Chatham Empire of Varieties, and even then his fee for a week was forty pounds! Sadly, in later years, his failing health forced him to live in a warmer climate. He moved to Santa Cruz, in Tenerife, but still managed a yearly visit to Carlisle. His last was in 1965, when he spent a few days with his son Arthur. Before leaving he took a sad look at his beloved theatre, by then reduced to a bingo hall. He was never to see it again. He died in his sleep in 1966 in Santa Cruz. His body was flown back to London for cremation; his ashes were buried alongside his mother and father at Causeway Head Church in Silloth. The runaway chemist's apprentice had at last come home.

Lupino Lane made the Lambeth Walk a hit. His son Laurie married AC's daughter Kathleen

87

ROBERT ANDERSON

The Cumberland Bard from Carlisle

Fast-falling snowflakes pierced the early morning dark, fluttering like ghostly white butterflies in the lamplight spilled from a window of a tumbledown cottage in Carlisle's English Damside; a humble home standing amid a squalor of tumbledown weaving sheds and sitting beside a road that was nothing more than a sea of winter mud.

It was the first day of February, 1770, and it was six o'clock in the morning. From the house with the lighted window, just one of many packed beneath the city's West Walls, came the wail of a newborn child. Inside the house Old Goody Isbel, the midwife, pursed her lips. The baby was small and a weakling. Isbel shook her head and tut-tutted. This one would not live long.

How wrong she was! The baby boy thrived, to grow into the man known as the Bard of Cumberland, a gifted man who, despite his early lack of learning, became a prolific balladeer. Robert Anderson was to pen some 200 ballads, nearly all in dialect that were, in fact, a definitive chronicle of life and customs of the county.

The Whitehaven Herald, reviewing an edition of his Cumberland Ballads, said: "As a portrayer of rustic manners, as a relator of homely incident, as hander-down of ancient customs and ways of life fast wearing or worn out, as an exponent of the feelings, tastes, habits and language of the most interesting class in a most interesting district, and in some other respects, we hold Anderson to be unequalled, not in Cumberland only, but in England. "As a description of a long, rapid, and varied succession of scenes, occurring at a gathering of country people intent upon enjoying themselves in their own uncouth roistering fashion, given in rattling, jingling, regularly irregular rhymes, with a chorus that is of itself a concentration of uproarious

Robert Anderson in pensive mood

English Damside today. Railway arches and walls stand on the spot where Anderson was born

fun and revelry, we have never read or heard anything like Anderson's 'Worton Wedding'." The National Dictionary of Biography says of him: "Anderson drew his materials from real life, was much feared for his personal attacks, had a keen eye for the ludicrous, and pictured with fidelity the ale-drinking, guzzling, and cock-fighting side of the Cumbrian farm labourer."

This cynical perception of his fellow men was instanced in an unpublished poem that he titled 'Lines written on being in company with a set of drunken brutes in Carlisle'. It read:

Now oft into company mortals will fall,
Where rudeness and impudence seem to please all;
Obscenity, scandal, vice, folly and pride
Is daily, ev'n hourly, a vile creature's guide;
To quarrel, swear, lie, oft to fight's their delight,
With joy contradicting whatever is right
The man of base mind ever glories in strife
The rash, the impetuous, bring ruin to life.

Later, as an accomplished musician - he played German flute and became a member of the Edenside Rangers' military band - he must have felt justified in writing what he called "Extempore Lines to the worst singer I ever heard"! They read :
Sweet is the screech-owl's harshest notes,
Compar'd with murm'rings from thy throat;
Nay, with more pleasure could I hear
The growlings of a hungry bear;
And sooner, far, the brute would be,
Than doom'd to sit and listen thee!

Robert Anderson used to say of the day that he was born: "I was a poor little tender being, scarce worth the trouble of rearing. Old Isbel, who assisted at the birth of hundreds, entertained fears that I was sent only to peer around me and leave them to shed tears for my loss."

No time was lost christening the babe. "'Ere twelve times I had seen the light, to the church they hurried me." Adam Anderson and his wife Frances had their son christened on February 4, 1770, at St Mary's Church. Now long gone, it stood to the left of the entrance to the Cathedral and was the city's parish church.

Anderson, recalling his early days, said: "I was the youngest of nine children born of parents getting up in years, who, with all their kindred, had been kept in bondage by poverty, hard labour, and crosses." As the youngest he was his mother's pet. "Well do I remember the fond caresses of my beloved mother. Oft did I get the odd halfpenny to spend that could ill be spared, besides experiencing indulgences unknown to my brothers and sisters."

At an early age Robert was found a place in the charity school supported by the Dean and Chapter of the cathedral that backed on to West Walls. He recalled: "Still do I remember the neat dress, slow speech, placid countenance, nay, every feature of good old Mrs Addison, the teacher." Mrs Addison taught reading and plain sewing, two subjects that Anderson thought would make so much difference to the future of her young pupils. But there were to be times when he was happily absent from the classroom; he was later to recall: "Having studied my letters, the see-saw drone of the 'Primer' and waded through the 'Reading Made Easy' and 'Dyche's Spelling Book' I was now turned over to a long, lean, needy Pretender to Knowledge. His figure was similar to that of the mad knight of La Mancha (Never have I perused that inexhaustible treasury of humour without having my tutor in view) "Free from the rod I spent those happy days with not much profit to myself in anything except writing, the rudiments of which I learned from his instructions."

The young Anderson was to spend more time beside a river than in a classroom. He said: "Impelled, probably, by necessity, he devoted so much time to angling that his few, starved-looking scholars were shamefully neglected. As for me, learning could not be considered very irksome with this master. He always selected me to accompany him on his piscatorial expeditions, up the banks of the Eden or the Caldew, on which I had a double duty to perform. First to carry the speckled trout and silver fry, a duty of which I was not a little proud; and secondly to gather my master various herbs, such as Colt's Foot, Betony and Ground Ivy; these he used as a substitute for tea, a substitution, which it may be observed, his poverty and not his inclination induced him to adopt." Carefree days for Robert. But not an ideal education. His parents could not read, but, ahead of their time and conscious of the need, delighted in others learning so to do.

"Finding I did not make progress equal to their expectations they placed me in the Quakers' School under Mr Isaac Ritson, a very learned and ingenious man."

Robert Anderson's education was to be sadly curtailed. His mother had died, and at the age of ten he had to leave and find work, wages desperately needed took precedence over schooling. "It was found necessary that I should quit school, in order to try and earn a little by hard labour wherewith to assist my poor father who had now become infirm."

He soon found employment, working with one of his brothers, a calico printer. "At the end of the first week well do I remember the happiness it afforded me to present my wages, one shilling, to my beloved father. Besides, putting a few pence in my pocket it caused me to be looked up to by my companions, and also enabled me to procure, occasionally, from a library, the works of Addison, Pope, Fielding, Smollett and others; but the perusal of poetry gave me the greatest pleasure."

Robert stayed with the calico printers for three years, and in 1783

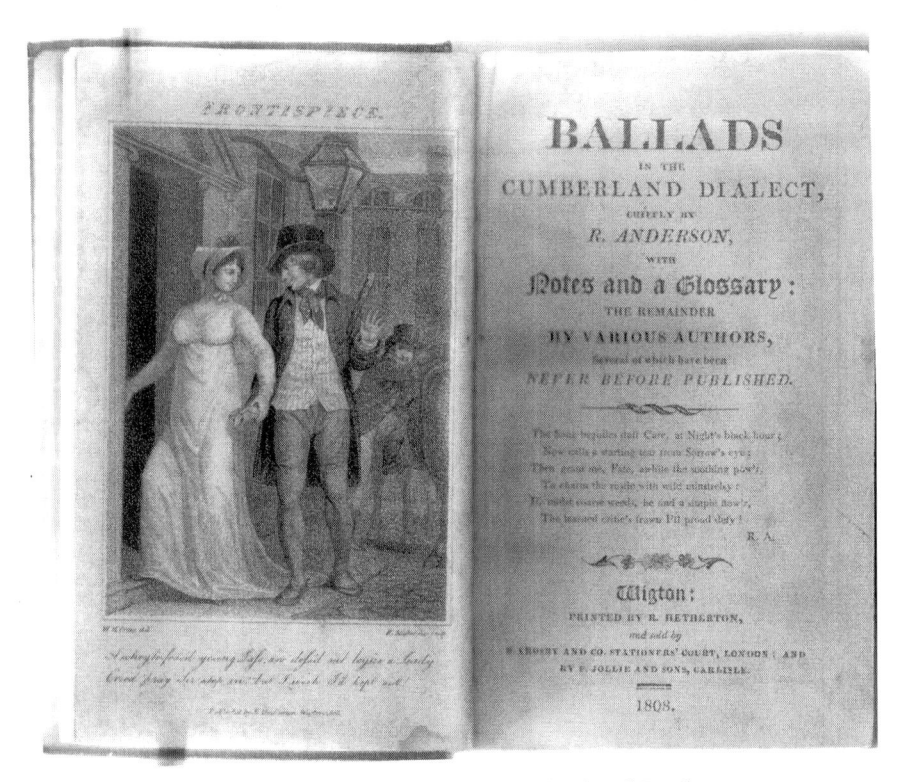

*Title page of Ballads in the Cumberland Dialect
published in Wigton in 1808*

became an apprentice pattern drawer with T.Losh and Company, in Dentonholme. Losh and Company's cotton stampery stood by the mill race at Holme Head, Thomas Losh had as partners John Milbourne, Thomas Benson, George Mounsey and John Wasdale.

It was at this time his father, despite his illness and poverty, somehow gathered together enough cash to buy his son a German flute and Robert started to study music. He was to remember: "This instrument has soothed my harassed mind during many an hour of sorrow." He quickly mastered the instrument, amusing his neighbours and his friends. Strollers along the banks of the rivers Caldew or Eden would stop and listen, entranced by the liquid notes floating to them on the evening breeze.

Said Robert: "But my greatest joy was to please a parent who delighted in old Scottish airs which I have often played for him."

He had first heard traditional Scottish airs as a boy, when he ran errands for the old lady who lived next door. In 1870, a Mrs Fisher, speaking at a soiree in Carlisle celebrating the centenary of his birth, said that she had little doubt that it was the old Highland woman who was a neighbour of his father and who used to repeat over in the Winter evenings to her young and ardent listener the old Scotch ballads of Gilderoy, Sir James The Ross and others who first awakened in Anderson's mind the love of song. There were to be other loves! His diary is littered with names and appointments with women. The first occasion was on one of the Sundays he spent roaming the countryside surrounding the city. Robert fell for a pretty face. He was just sixteen. The girl was younger. He even considered marriage! Later he told the tale: "It was on paying a visit at a friend's house that I was first smitten with female charms, which produced such an effect on me that I cannot now understand? Picture a diffident youth in his sixteenth year daily pouring out the sighs of a sincere heart for an artless, rosy cottager somewhat younger than myself.

"At church she attracted all my attention and occupied that place in my thoughts which I ought to have allotted to the preacher. Had my income, which was then barely sufficient to procure the necessities of life, been more adequate, with what happiness could I have laid my fortunes at her feet and offered myself to her for better or for worse, but fate decreed otherwise." It was the first instance of Anderson losing his head to a woman. It was to happen again and again, especially in his later years in Northern Ireland where, once more, he would pour his heart out to no avail.

In 1791 he left behind the rural delights of Cumberland and set off for the bright lights of London. In one way it was not the best of moves. Said he: "Unfortunately I had engaged myself to a wretch of the most unprincipled character. I was compelled to arrest him for my wages, and the distress occasioned me by his villainy was of no inconsiderable amount."

Short of money, Robert was forced to find the cheapest accommodation and subsist on a starvation diet. There almost never was a bard of Cumberland! Recalling those unhappy days he said: "For some months I was confined to a wretched garret, and but for the kindness of a sister I must have perished of want and misery."

But fortune eventually smiled on him. He found another job with a more amenable employer. He was fulsome in his praise: "Fortunately I afterwards got employment under a master as remarkable for his goodness as my former one had been remarkable for his wickedness. By him I was used more like a companion than a servant."

There was to be more good news for Robert, for it was in London that he first found songwriting success. "In 1794, being in Vauxhall Gardens for the first time I felt myself disgusted with many of the songs written in the mock pastoral Scottish style, and, supposing myself capable of producing what might be considered equal, or, perhaps, superior, on the following day wrote four songs. Lucy Grey was my first attempt and was suggested on hearing a Northumbrian rustic relating the story of two lovers. The songs were set to music by Mr Hook and my first poetic effusion was sung by Master Phelps, with great applause."

Lucy Gray was one of the songs that, much later, he had included in a collection dedicated to Mrs Henry Howard, of Corby Castle. The Henry Howard who commanded the Edenside Rangers - and who was related to the Duke of Norfolk - knew of Robert's musical and verse-writing talents, and he was on their acceptable social list. On Monday, February 29, 1808, he received an invitation from Corby Castle that read: "Mrs Howard presents her compliments to Mr Anderson, and as there is to be some Festivity downstairs tomorrow evening, should Mr Anderson like to join the party at six o'clock, he will be welcome to a bed."

After meeting her at a musical evening at the castle he had recorded: "Had some conversation with Mrs Howard, one of the most pleasant women I have long conversed with. She seems particularly fond of the lighter studies..." If he was mixing with the nobility the next day would have brought him down to earth: "Very ill all day, and to add to my miseries received Bills that I am unable to discharge.

In a footnote to the collection he was to tell Mrs Howard how he had been inspired to write it: "This rural trifle was the author's first poetical attempt, and with five others equally simple, was offered to his friend Mr Hook, composer and manager of Vauxhall Gardens. The whole were set to

Vauxhaul Pleasure gardens as depicted by Thomas Rowlandson

music and sung by Mr Dignum, Mr Taylor, Mrs Mountain, Miss Franklin and Master Phelps in 1794. The last mentioned person closed the season with the song in question.

"The author, in London, heard a rustic relate in artless manner the story of the unfortunate lovers which gave rise to the ballad. Lucy was the toast of the neighborhood, and to use his uncouth language 'monie a canny lad wad hae travelled miles after dark, aye, thro' fire and water, just to get a gliff on her' James Walton, a neighboring farmer's son, from his wonderful agility as a dancer, proved the hero of Lucy's attention. Disease, the canker worm, prey'd on her damask cheek, and this blooming bud withered and died in her seventeenth year. James seldom spoke afterwards, but haunted the favourite seat in a dell near the burn and e're long, according to request, was laid by the side of his Lucy."

The song went:
Say, have you seen the blushing rose,

The blooming pink or lily pale?
Fairer than any flow'r that blows,
Was Lucy Gray of Allendale.

Pensive at eve, down by the burn,
Where oft the maid they used to hail,
The shepherds now are heard to mourn,
For Lucy Gray of Allendale.

With her to join the sportive dance,
Far have I stray'd o'er hill and vale;
Then, pleas'd, each rustic stole a glance
At Lucy Gray of Allendale.

I, sighing, view yon hawthorn shade,
Where first I told a lover's tale;
For now low lays the matchless maid,
Sweet Lucy Gray of Allendale.

I cannot toil and seldom sleep;
My parents wonder what I ail:
While others rest, I wake and weep,
For Lucy Gray of Allendale.

A load of grief preys on my breast,
In cottage or in darken'd vale;
Come, welcome Death! O' let me rest
Near Lucy Gray of Allendale!

The first to hear Anderson's Lucy Grey were those strolling in Vauxhall Gardens, the premier pleasure garden of eighteenth century London. Those who could afford it wandered along tree-lined avenues, from all sides serenaded by music. Fifty years before Anderson walked the leafy arbours the cost of admission was high. It was a shilling, no small amount of money.

The assistance with Lucy Grey came from no amateurs. Mr Hook proved to be James Hook, a famous composer of the time. His Sweet Lass of Richmond Hill is sung to this day!

Hook's first position was that of organist at White Conduit House, Pentonville, one of the many tea gardens that abounded in eighteenth century London. He made a name for himself not only as an organist and a teacher, but also as a composer of light, attractive music. He wrote more than 2,000 songs, most of which were for specific singers at the London pleasure gardens, notably for Vauxhall. Their catchy melodies would have been immediately appealing to the Vauxhall crowds.

There was to be another pleasant surprise for Robert. His father, now aged seventy six, called to see him.

Surely Robert had got that wrong! A seventy-six-year old man walking fifty miles a day! He had walked the 301 miles from Carlisle to London in six days! He recalled: "Tears of joy greeted our meeting, but such was his aversion to the noise and tumult of London that I could only prevail upon him to remain with me seven days, at the end of which he returned to Carlisle."

It was in 1794, whilst he was living in London that Anderson wrote a short piece he called "The Mendicant" Again he mentions a woman. This time a mysterious Eliza was apparently yet another woman without whom he could not live. Or was she his literary invention?

He wrote: "It was not in Grosvenor Square, Hanover Square, Cavendish Square or Portland Place, but in St James' Park where I saw him.

"One of those light, refreshing showers which enliven the face of nature in the month of May, had for some time confined me to my gloomy apartment. Through the patched lattice of which (it being an attic, or poet's parlour) I could

James Hook who set Anderson's words to music

only behold a rainbow which formed a broad arch over the proud Metropolis, and seemed to laugh at all the puny pigmies men call artists. "Well thou knowest Eliza, my bad state of health demands both air and exercise; but I fear that thy absence will add to my weakness. Return, sweet bud of innocence! Lest soon the withered leaves may rustle over my last and narrow dwelling.

"The clouds having for a few hours having been spitting at the diminutive city of London now began to threaten vengeance on the strong men of Kent; when I ventured along Pall Mall and seated myself near that ancient fabric, whose owner, the most wretched of his subjects need not envy. "For me Eliza, thy company in the meanest cottage on the most barren plot of earth would make me happier than any mortal born to wear a crown at the expense of millions kept in slavery.

"The clock at the Horse Guards struck seven: the hour, thought I, resting one elbow on the arm of the seat and looking steadfastly to the ground; the hour when Eliza bade me adieu as the coach left. I had been reading thy last letter, and was looking around, afraid some might perceive me kissing (Call me not childish, Eliza, for fancying I kissed the rose on thy cheek) when I was accosted by one whose look and address told me he had known better days. An observer of mankind can always perceive, whether meek virtue, or riot drunk vice prompts the wretched to solicit charity; and as I immediately set him down as one of the first order of beings my heart sympathised with him and I could have wiped away the tears stealing down his furrowed face as he approached within three paces of my seat. 'Sir,' he said in one of those musical and melancholy tones of supplication which ought ever to rivet the attention of those who struggle against misfortune, 'Pardon one who is forced to beg the relief he lately gave to others. In vain do I knock at the doors of the rich; those who know not distress too pity the wretched; and I venture to solicit charity where the heart joins the hand of the giver. I have seen much of the busy world; and lived in affluence cherishing the summer flies by whom f am now neglected and despised. Pardon me, Sir! My story would be long and tedious.'

"He ceased, and turned from me to hide the working of his painful bosom. I am no physiognomist, Eliza, but without having studied the essays of Lavater could read in his look that he stood little indebted to mankind.

Who knows, thought I, somewhat enraged on finding one pocket sans cash; who knows but the Father of the universe, and himself, the sufferings of that virtuous being? May not his distress be owing to those who bask in the sunshine of plenty, living on their country's ruin?

"Perhaps war and its numberless train of evils may have driven him from the commercial world, without a friend or a shelter from the storm. `Be upon thy guard! muttered Jealousy at that moment. Thou art poor!', whispered Pride, `and what thou wouldst give him might ornament thy dress'‛ "No matter, thought 1, seeing a tear fall down his pale cheek; no matter! There is a pleasure in softening the wretchedness of a brother, unknown to you all; and in this short image of life shall man, when he beholds an aged and infirm one bowed down by Poverty, and faint, and weary, and helpless, and broken, thrown amidst thorns by the wayside; shall he jog at a proud pace without trying to help the suffering traveller...

"I gazed, and at that moment his eyes met mine with a look seeming to say, `Let sorrow be to you unknown and plenty be thy portion!' "Just then I thought of what had just fallen from your lips, Eliza, 'Tis a hard heart that chides the hand for relieving age in want!"'... Robert, continued to harangue those who would pass by a`poor, aged, implorer of mercy'. It could well have done duty as a sermon from any pulpit. He ended with a warning: "Remember, you may, ere long, be summoned before Him who shall judge the world; who hath commanded by his servants, that you do unto all as you would they should do unto you!" He had obviously intended his words for publication adding a footnote that read: "Mr Ed, this tale which may be admired but by few of your readers, is founded on fact, written partly in the style of Sterne". Robert left London in October, 1796, and, at his father's wish, returned to Cumberland. He explained: "His letters stated him to be unhappily situated; and that duty which had prompted me from infancy made me fly to his assistance."

By this time a skilled textile worker, he easily found work again, this time joining Lamb, Scott, Foster and Company. He said: "The situation thus obtained in my native place proved in every sense agreeable. I experienced from friends who now became numerous, every proof of esteem. " By now he had written a great number of poetical pieces, and in 1798 he published a volume of poems. It failed to make him a profit. Ruefully he recalled: "From this publication I received little more than dear-bought praise; for numbers of my subscribers never paid their subscriptions. It was sent to the press under the title of "Cumberland Ballads. The receipts were barely sufficient to defray the expenses of publication; much of the subscription money being lost. The work, however, became somewhat popular, and the edition was soon exhausted; and a new impression was sent into the world from the press of Mr Hetherton, of Wigton, who purchased the copyright." However, Mr Hetherton did not remain long in the print business, in 1813 it was owned by one E. Rook. They seemed to be queuing up to publish Robert's Cumberland Ballads, for in 1815 Rook reprinted Hetherton's edition.

His diary revealed days filled with pastimes and pleasures, endeavours and pithy comment. There were also financial worries. As the last days of 1800 ticked away and a new century approached, Robert was struggling to keep up with his debts. Christmas was not to be a merry one. "Dec 25: Arose without one coin in my pocket; and doubt this will be the poorest week I have known since I first joined the social pleasures of Christmas, and I had promised myself to spend a week's happiness, hoping for the payment of money due for teaching, to have discharged everything and rested in peace, but he who trusts tomorrow deserves to go without, if it be in his power to provide today. Dined with Mr Gibbons and drank heartily, not for what I drank but to forget myself. Invited for tea and supper with _____ , but could not make one for the reasons above."

On New Year's Eve he dined with friends and ended the day in a better humour: laughed away a couple of hours at Jossie's." Twenty four hours later the gloom descended once again.

"January 1, 1801. A new century. Began with an unpleasant circumstance, my father means to quit his lodgings; had a most painful interview with him this morning. O' that I had a comfortable spot of my own to take him to!" His despair soon lifted. The very next day he started work at the Printfield and was earning the money he needed so much.

On January 3 he noted: "Called on my Father and contributed to his happiness. Thank God he seems comfortably situated, nay, doubtless he might really be so; were it not that age makes him childish. Spent this evening at Jossies."

Life was following its usual pattern, Robert again on the receiving end of abuse. "Jan 5. Spent this evening pleasantly at Mr J's and heard there of Miss (name heavily erased) behaviour respecting my friend Hodgson and myself. Curse on the tongue of that malignant, noisy, monster that constantly traffics this slander. I long have wished to abuse this ugly wretch and expose her as a liar, but dare not on account of my informer."

January 9 saw another of his mysterious entries: "Called to see Miss X, but was sorry afterwards for a particular reason." His social whirl continued, but the quality of his company was questionable. "January 21, spent the evening with an uproarious set of dunces. Two days later: "Drank tea at Mrs Pearson's where Miss Gilpin was one of the party, whose easy cheerfulness and humourous songs, sung in so great a style, made this one of the pleasantest evenings I have for some time spent."

Catherine Gilpin, the lady whose cheerfulness had so impressed Robert, was also a poet, and the devoted friend of Susanna Blamire, another, more gifted poet. Until Susanna's early death at the age of 47, they had shared a house at 14, Finkle Street, and wrote lyrics together. Susanna was born in 1747 at Caldew Hall, near Dalston. She played guitar, with which she often entertained her guests, an was often to be found composing songs in the woodland glades around Raughtonhead.

Mary Slee, in a booklet published in 1917 to raise funds for the Cumberland Infirmary, described Susanna as possessing the most original and reflective mind that Cumberland had ever produced excepting William Wordsworth.

Later Robert saw his brother, heard that he had been paid off, and immediately started to seek other work for him. "Applied to Mr G for work." The next day he heard that his brother had failed to find employment at the Old Printfield, and once more went into action, taking him to the Woodbank print works just outside the village of Brisco, some three miles south of the city. With some satisfaction he noted: "He got immediate work." In an age when few ventured abroad, and even then restricting their travels to France and Italy, he was privileged to hear some rare travel stories on 27 February, 1801: " Drank tea with Mr and Mrs C and spent a pleasant couple of hours with Mr D who recounted his travels to Egypt, Jerusalem, Constantinople.

Sunday 28: "Dined at Mrs Johnston's and took possession of my old apartment; but what a change do I feel in the loss of Mr J. Spent the evening at Jossies among the 'rory Tory' boys.

March 3: "Read Goldsmith's pleasant comedy of `She Stoops To Conquer', and was agreeably entertained with the natural simplicity of some of the characters as also the wit of this distinguished man."

On August 26th he was at the annual Carlisle Great Fair. "Drank tea with Miss R, Miss T and Miss L, with the last of whom I loitered an hour away in a dancing room."

The following day found him writing: "Fell in with a new married couple and dined and drank tea at Mr P's, where all was merriment and drunkenness." Nor surprisingly the next day's diary noted: "Sunday, 28th. In bed most of the day quite fatigued."

He keeps us guessing with an entry for September 1, 1801; "Saw her I like best this day but had not an opportunity of speaking to her." Yet another mysterious woman? But the next few days found him recording the more serious side of his life.

"Called to see my father who has again changed his lodging and come to Carlisle, where he frets and is for ever unhappy."

Robert lived in the days when executions were part of everyday public entertainment, when crowds would gather at Carlisle's gaol to watch the unfortunates hang. September 3: "Saw Mansfield executed, who behaved with the greatest fortitude imaginable. Spent two or three hours with Crito." Crito was the name he gave to one of his best friends, Thomas Sanderson, another poet, who lived at Kirklinton, who was to encourage and inspire him.

September 5th found him, not having any work, "reading Tristram Shandy all day". Laurence Sterne was obviously one of his favourite authors.

Then the diary returns to more of the pleasant distractions of life. September 9: Joined the Cumberland Rangers at the request of my friends." The next day he recorded: "Spent an irregular night with Wilkinson. Drank tea with Miss R and spent two hours with a sweet good girl, the Bonnie Bird. Robert had really fallen for the young lady. Two days later found him writing: "A day of idleness but a night of pleasure saw my Bonny bird and wish I could press her to my bosom and say thou art mine." Maybe that's why the next day he was noting: "Heard Mr Fawcett preach an excellent sermon on forgiveness of sins."

Did the ladies have some fatal attraction for Robert? Names - or just their initials - pop up page after page in his diary. "Met Miss A and with her called to see Blanche, the sprightliest, bewitching little devil I ever knew, with a pair of bright peepers enough to make a saint forget his devotion. Had a long walk with her to Newtown and wish I were wealthy for her sake. Military duties called him on September 13: "Appeared with the band in full uniform before Lieutenant Colonels Howard and Wallace." September 15th saw him spending two hours with the Bonnie Bird, "an enchanting lass." Later in 1801 he was on his social rounds again, and once more eying up the ladies: "Oct 8. Drank tea at Miss R's where the finest girl I ken was of the party, saw her home and wished her my ain thing." The next day he had to deal with the more serious side of life. "Hired a horse for my nephew, who is dying, and went with him to take the advice of Dr Blamire of Hawkesdale."

A brief respite from troubles and illness came on October 10: Wrote a long letter to a dear girl in London." Sunday of that week he was again playing the Good Samaritan and, in reflective mood, writing: "I spent the evening with poor Embleton in the jail, and much I fear will be my situation 'ere many years have rolled over my head."

Robert constantly worried about the health if his father and was always the dutiful son. "October 21. Sent for by my father who is exceeding ill; and am afraid of an approaching dissolution. Called in the evening and found him better." Four days later: "Sent for by Miss Dacre about my father, and can never forget his goodness." His worries were needless, Adam Anderson was to live for another six years.

On November 6 intrigue returned to the pages of his diary with an entry over which there can only be conjecture: "Called on _____ according to appointment and spent a pleasant hour, but discovered something which caused much uneasiness."

On November 9 Robert was taking up arms for one of his friends: "Wrote a long letter to Sir W. Lawson for poor Carlyle, who, I am sorry to say, is ill=treated by the senseless sycophants who surround this great little man. I hope the lines of truth, tho' given in an unconnected manner, will convince this pretended admirer of services, that he, like too many, wishes to play the tyrant."

Robert had always taken a keen interest in the manners and dialect of the Cumbrian farm workers, and it came as no surprise that, in December

1801, he published a ballad called Betty Brown, written in the Cumbrian dialect. "Betty Brown" told the story of Gweordie, a lovesick rustic, turning down the chance to go to Rosley Fair with his friend Wully. The first stanza read:

Come Gweordie lad, unyoke the yad,
Let's gow to Rosley Fair
Lang Ned's afwore, wi Symie's lad,
Peed Dick, and monie mair:
My titty Greace and Jenny Bell
Are gangen bye and bye,
Sae doff thy clogs, and don thyself -
Let fadder luik to t'kye

If the dialect was often difficult to understand readers of Anderson always had the faithful George Crowther, who later laboriously penned what was essentially a Cumbrian Dialect/English Language Dictionary!

Gweordie replies:
0, Wully leetsome may ye be!
For me, I downa gang;
I've often shek'd a leg with thee,
But now I's aw queyte wrang;
My stomach's gean, nae sleep I get;
At neet I lig me down,
But nobbut pech, and gowl, and fret'
And aw for Betty Brown."

Said Robert: "The praise bestowed by many, but particularly my valued friend Thomas Sanderson, himself a poet of no mean pretensions, encouraged me to other attempts in the same species of poetry. At length a sufficient number of these pieces were produced to form a volume." On October 15, 1801, Robert had written: "Had two hours conversation with Crito, who advises me to publish my Cumberland Ballads." Sanderson, who lived at Kirklinton, and whom Robert met in 1795, was to be a life-long friend. The Reverend Thomas Torver, who, in 1904, edited an edition of Robert's ballads, said: "Crito, or Sanderson, seems to have been to him in Cumberland what Andrew Mackenzie was to him in Ireland, at once a literary collabarateur and a firm and unfailing friend." Sadly Sanderson was later to burn to death when, in January 1829, his house accidentally caught fire

Another note in Robert's diary read: "June 5. Fell in with Crito, who dined with me; afterwards we took a ramble around the town to mark the strange country characters this day drawn together. Enjoyed with my abstemious friend a hearty glass; and what is equally uncommon had a range round the dancing room with him."

Drinking and dancing they may have been, but at times Sanderson was not the merriest of poets. Thinking over the loss of friends and companions of his youth he wrote this verse in his "Lay", dedicated to his native village:

And blest are you in early graves,
For age is but protracted pain;
A longer strife with winds and waves,
Upon a wild and windy main.
My lot has been to linger hgere,
Till every earthly joy has fled;
Till all is gone the heart holds dear,
And gathered sorrows bow my head.

Said the Reverend Ellwood: "Of Anderson's style of writing in the Dialect, Sanderson, probably one of the most competent critics who ever wrote of this, has the following testimony: "His Cumberland Ballads display uncommon merit, and may be considered the most perfect specimens of pastoral writing that have yet appeared.

"The author has taken a wider view of rural life than any of his predecessors, and has been more happy in describing the peculiar cast of thought and expression by which individual manners are distinguished. In delineating the character of the peasantry he has closely adhered to nature and truth, never raising them above their condition by too much refinement and never depressing them below it by too much vulgarity. He holds them up often to laughter, but never contempt. He has the happy talent of catching the ludicrous in everything that comes before him and expressing it with that facility which gives its full force to the reader."

But life for Robert Anderson was not all spent writing ballads and strolling the river banks of Carlisle; he had other pursuits more in keeping with those of a single, 32 year old man living in the city.

In September, 1801, his diary noted: "Called to see my unhappy father and left without a shilling in the world. Attended parade." September 30: "Wrote a sonnet to poverty, but not liking it lighted my pipe with it. Spent the evening with my father."

October 1. "Loitered the afternoon away in drunkenness..."

October 23rd saw him taking tea with three ladies. "We had a pleasant chat." Another entry for the same day read: "Met a female friend who I met by appointment, whom I shall not forget."

He was a member of the Edenside Rangers, the volunteer Militia force that had Henry Howard, of Corby Castle, in command. It was a time when Napoleon Bonaparte was a bogey man that many feared might invade Britain. An entry in his diary for December 1801, reads: "Attended with the Edenside Rangers at the Castle; afterwards at the Bitts here a concorde of people were assembled to see the shooting match for prizes given by Mr Howard. The first, 10/6d and a knife, was won by R. Boustead. The second, 5/©, won by Jos Foster. Got tipsy like all the rest in the evening."

Robert had a busy New Year's Eve. December 31: "Walked to Cummersdale in the morning. Spent the afternoon in idleness. Supped with the Band and a few friends at Foster's; and played in the New Year."

The next day he wrote: "January 1, 1802: Began the New Year by working all day. Called on in the evening by a smart female, wishing me to make one of a party. Would to God she had been (indecipherable) or ten years younger then this would have been a happy night."

Later that year he heard sad news of Charles Johnston, a great friend. "May 7, Mr Johnston very ill all day."

The next day: "Mr J worse and confined to his bed. God grant his complaint may not be of a feverish nature on account of his small family."

While concerned with the health of his friend, he had been ignoring his own, and on May 9th received a stern warning: "Sent for by Doctor James, who requested me immediately to seek another lodging, telling me that I was dangerously ill of a fever; his son Henry was yesterday taken ill and is worse this day." Robert, aware of the great number infected by the fever, obeyed orders. Left the house and went to Mr Gibson's."

Seven days later there was even worse news. Johnston, a fellow Freemason and a fellow member of the Edenside Rangers, had died.

"14th. Heard at seven this morning of Mr Johnston's death which happened at six. Went immediately to Wigton where most of the inhabitants seem much affected on hearing the melancholy news. Alas! What a distressed state are his family in. Mr Stamper and Mr Lowry returned with me to Carlisle. Drank tea with them at the Coffee House. Attended in the evening at Armstrong's where the friends and neighbours of the deceased attended in the corpse house. Gave orders for the funeral. Saw Mr Howard who commanded the Eden Rangers to attend."

The next day found him making the final preparations for the funeral. "Sent for at twelve by Mr S. At two the corpse of my friend was lifted and attended to St Cuthbert s by the Freemasons (both Lodges) the Edenside Rangers and a great concourse of people. who all bore melancholy testimony of the solemn spectacle. After the corpse was interred three volleys were fired by the Rangers. the three youngest children were christened; to the eldest I stood Godfather."

The next day he had to deal with family worries: "15th. Drank tea with my father at Newtown: where he will next remove I cannot conjecture." Robert's social lifestyle was no more evident than on four consecutive May days in 1802. 21st. Spent the evening at the Bowling Green. Drank tea with two ladies. 22nd. Walked to Aikton in the evening with Pearson and Lowry. Had buttered sops, brandy, vocal and instrumental music, conversation, etc., till past the hour of midnight."

It would have been a filling meal. Sops consisted of slices of bread soaked in melted butter and sugar, stirred to a thick consistency and eaten with a spoon.

Sunday, 23rd. Joined in our party by Mr How and a Mr Dand, both men of good sense. Went to church where I heard for the first time a clarinet accompany the vocal, but uncultivated melodists, and was not a little pleased with the effect it produced - cannot help thinking two bassoons and two clarinets, with the four vocal parts would be more solemn to my ear than of the finest performance, even of an Arnold or Joan Bates. Spent this afternoon with real pleasure in a company where cheerfulness, shrewd observation, humorous anecdote and the social glass made all happy. Reached Carlisle about half past eight."

24th. Lord Lonsdale died. Copied four songs. Called to see my father."

On May 28th he was furious, the pages of the diary must have been smouldering as he described that which had angered him. Following the death of Johnston he had been organising a concert to raise funds for the widow and her family. Now there seemed to be some opposition: "Provoked in the evening by the insolence of that nasty, sottish-faced, superannuated ignoramus Glendinning, who threatened to stop the performance. Curse on him! May he be double, double damned in the next world nor ever taste happiness in this, who would injure the widow and her helpless family, but I trust the views of this stupid standby will be counteracted by a generous public." All seemed well the next day: "Heard with pleasure of the Masons granting leave for the performance."

The diary entries recording his charitable efforts were interrupted, for once the ladies were talking about Robert! "June 2. Heard of Miss C abusing me; and mean to drop this lying hussey a pretty sharp letter ere long." But the charity concert, for which he had been selling tickets, was still very much on his mind. "June 6, Exceeding ill all day. Saw with great pleasure the signs of a good Benefit."

The following day he met some of the artistes who were to take part. "Met at three in the afternoon my friend Jemmy Grant; who with Mr and Mrs Trumpton, Miss Biggs, Mrs and Miss Walstein then arrived, Drank tea with them and had a great deal of chat with Mr G, who was quite overjoyed at the appearance of the house being a bumper, which was really the case; for never have I seen a room so full of people. Heard enraptured the sweet voice of Miss Walstein whose songs would almost turn a saint from his devotion; but could not enjoy the performance of the rest, being a doorkeeper, against my mind. Supped with this little theatrical corps, who were all happy in being so well received by such an audience."

June 8: "Breakfasted with above and saw them safely coached for Liverpool where I wish them success. Being unfit for work, took a ramble to Newtown and spent the afternoon in the Bowling Green." The Bowling Green, the inn at the Springfield Gardens end of Lowther Street, was one of his favourite haunts.

The next few months saw him once again enjoying the attentions of the ladies - although delighting in one beauty two others in the company

109

certainly did not appeal to him!

August 2. "Made one of a tea party at Mr B's where a young lady made me forget a late determination, viz, never to fall in love. Heard a great many new songs sung with taste; and but for an old woman lately converted by the Methodical corps, and a young Old Maid who has just discovered that cheerfulness merits eternal punishment, this truly would have been a happy night."

The next day he was writing: "Heard of an enquiry a certain female has made about me. Played in the evening a hand of cribbage with Mr G."

Then Robert was back to his theatrical breast-beating: "Dreamt last night of happiness I must never enjoy, which made an impression on my mind. Wrote for Miss B`The Beggar Girl; who called and got it with two more. I admire this lively little creature but dare not, for the soul of me, own it. Good Heavens! Shall man smother the noblest flame that fires his bosom? Yes, such are the trammels sanctioned by custom that even the soft passion of love is too often deemed criminal. Saw her home."

In an age when propriety seemed always to be observed Robert's next diary entry, had it been made public, would surely have lifted a few eyebrows: "10 th. Called to see ____ with whom I spent an hour in her bedchamber, forsooth, but with more disgust than affection; and shall never forget the interrogatories of this night."

August was a busy months for him: 11th. "Called and played a few rounds of cards with the Misses N's. Heard this night of a story of Hodgson's behaviour which really astonished me; and think him a proud, insolent, ungrateful puppy, for his treatment of an amiable old friend; but such characters are every day to be met with, and I have done with him."

12th "Received a line from Crito about the criticism of his poems. Attended at Fosters according to promise; where a few wrangling blockheads meet without any knowledge of music, or yet decorum." 13th. "Called in the evening to see my father who is awkwardly situated and will always be unhappy - saw the dear little girl that I love."

16th. "Heard Miss ____ sing `The Beggar Girl' in good style. Was informed by my good hostess of the envious remarks made by that gummy, ill-natured, canting thing of an old maid, Miss B."

18th. Spent an hour at Jossie's without pleasure, but a happy one in the company of her for whose esteem I would forfeit a kingdom. Cannot help thinking it will be my lot till I die."

"I admire this lively little creature ... dear little girl.... her for whose esteem he would give up a kingdom ... "

Were all the loving references to just one person? Surely not, for the amorous Robert was forever letting his eye wander!

The diary for August 19 reads: "Heard in the evening some memoirs of the sweet little miss I had the pleasure of walking home."

Then intrigue interrupted his sweet musing; was Robert harking back to the events of June 10, the day he entered a lady's bedchamber, when he wrote: "21st Called to see Miss X, who has forfeited my esteem for ever. O' vice of all vices that cannot be forgiven in a female!"

June brought more heartache. It was pure melodrama and his heart must have been aching as he wrote: "Heard what gave me pleasure but at the same time pain; Miss B esteems me more than any person, but the connection will not do, since whatever affection I might feel for this good girl, my scanty income and encumbered circumstances would prevent me from seeing her as I could wish. May she think more of a better and richer man." Once again poverty had thwarted him and perhaps it was that which spurred him, next day, into entering in his diary: "Wrote a line to that little venomous vixen who wantonly belied me to some of my best friends; told her character in six lines, which will prevent her from behaving so in future."

He was still grumpy and bitter a day later: "Saw a part of the 42nd or Highland Watch who arrived here this morning. Heard their band in the evening but have often listened to better performances."

So who was the young vixen who slandered Robert so? Certainly the pages of his diary give no clues, the ladies he meets are never mentioned by name. Typical is the entry that reads: "Saw the paragraph against Garrick with great pleasure. Drank tea with two unmarried ladies. Met ___."

The year 1803 opened boisterously. "Jan 5th. Attended at my nephew Carrick's footing, where where all peacable and snug; afterwards at Robert's son's footing where all was uproar and found myself affronted by Gibson, an ungrateful fellow, at whose house I have for six years spent much, and caused much to be spent, always having brought my friends there, nay, even everyone who met here this e'ening came on my account, but 'tis too often the case, were a man to spend a fortune with such he would, if poor, only be treated with contempt. Shall not forget this infamous treatment."

27th "Made one of Mrs T's party where a dance made me acquainted with some sweet damsels; and got Miss B for a partner with whom a connection might be advisable. Saw her home and appointed a meeting the next evening."

Next day: "Arose very ill from the over exertions of the preceding evening. Met Miss B."

Life was certainly varied for the man about the town. One Saturday saw him spending the day in "idle intoxication". The next day he "played the solemn dirge in the funeral procession of the unfortunate man who was killed on Friday. Drank tea at Mr A's." The following day he was seeing a young lady of his acquaintance"!

"Called on Miss Gilpin at noon and am to act as negotiator between her and Mr L. Called at Miss Atkinson" with her songs and music and chatted an hour."

But did this peep at their lifestyle tweak his conscience? He wrote: "Was quite hurt on thinking of my sister's miserable situation. Poor wretch, she left London where she was earning what supported her and a family to come here, where they are starving. O' that I should have been such a profligate as not to be enabled to assist her." This may have been Grace, the eldest Anderson girl, born in 1752 and surely was the sister who came to his rescue when he starved in a London garret.

The next day he was almost back to his more normal way of life: "Wrote the song 'I love a lass but dare not tell.' Invited to sup with the Dalston Brewery at the Pack Horse, but declined." Saying no to a brewery party was, to say the least, unusual for Robert!

Next day he was meeting his latest love: "Met Miss Graham with whom I had three hours chat; saw her home to Scotby and could not help noticing the gentle rebuke her mother gave her for staying at the town later than she used to do; but little did she know the cause. Feasted off honey bread and fresh butter, ale and gin and got home at seven. Promised to see her on Wednesday next at Scotby in the afternoon."

So who was Kate? She may have been another of his sisters, for the day after his dalliance with Miss G and meeting her family he wrote: "Spent an hour with Kate; and two at Mr Foster's where I was forced to get beastly drunk. Mean to treat Kate to the Mill's concert; and get her the `Song of the Thorn'" He also gave his Miss G a ticket, happily chatting with her and rejoicing in a parting kiss.

The following day was Shrove Tuesday, which he described as a holiday for blackguards and cockfighters. Wednesday was the day of his date with Miss B. It ended beyond all expectations!

"Walked to Scotby after dinner and kissed my rural queen who met me with joy beaming in her countenance. She spread the table with honey and the best country fare; and at five were joined by her parents who took great pains to make me happy in all the country affords. The girdle cake was made by Mary, and a dainty one it was, while the best of everything adorned the tea board. This beverage over we had along chat about anything marvellous, and a few of my Cumberland ballads were a great treat to the grand man and his dame. At eight I took leave and requested Mary to set me down the road; she blushed consent and walked near a mile when we mingled the chat of lovers with the sweetest kisses. She promised to go to the theatre with me on Saturday week; and I find I am more than half in love with her, and believe her to be a good girl, tho' without that excessive sensibility which is often pleasing and sometimes disgusting in a female. On my way home I meditated a song simply shewing in a wild manner the pleasures this rural scene afforded; it begins `I went to see my Mary...'

Countryside kisses could have been the reason why he reported a change of mood the following day: "Drank tea at the Mitchinsons, the following of the party; Mrs Pearson, Mrs Kennedy, Miss Gilpin, Miss Pearson, Miss Ward, Miss Graham, Miss Mitchinson, Mrs Mitchinson, Mr Pearson, and myself; and number this among the first evenings of my life; for the song, tale, anecdote and humour kept all alive. How seldom I have it in my power to share the pleasures of so polite a society; and when I am invited, it frequently happens that a sullen manner gets hold of me, and I hate myself, without being able to shake it off; but this evening I sat at ease and enjoyed the unusual flow of spirits."

November 6th saw him at the annual races on the Swifts. "Saw the race won by Cotillion. Spent the afternoon with Wilkinson, Strong, Hodgson and some others; the evening in dancing rooms where I saw one only that I would like to treat with."

Surprise, surprise! After a day at the races and a night spent dancing, the next day he noted: "Very ill from the debauch of last night. Wandered about all day. Drank tea with Lowry, Boustead and Hodgson." But he was well enough later to have a mysterious meeting: "Spent the evening at Jossie's. Met by appointment one who must be nameless."

Feb 21, 1803: "Read a long account of Colonel Despard's execution which affected me much. Wrote four songs for Miss Gilpin and drank tea with her and Mrs Goodeare; and had a pleasing three hours conversation. Wrote Ãletter to Miss G."

Colonel Despard, after an earlier brilliant career in the army, was executed for high treason. With a group of disaffected soldiers he had planned to seize the Tower of London and the Bank of England and to then assassinate the king!

One of Robert's best-loved ballads was that of the Bleckell Murry Neet. It was inspired by a visit to the White Ox on the city's Durdar road, where musicians and singers had gathered at the inn whose remarkable landlady was Mrs Nancy Dawson. Nancy ran the inn for sixty years, dying on March 3, 1844. On April 29, 1904, the Carlisle Patriot reported:

"Last week, when the earliest copies of the centenary edition were being issued from the press, workmen were demolishing the White Ox Public House which has become the property of the old Brewery Company, who intend erecting an up-to-date inn upon the site. The White Ox was the scene of the rustic revelry so graphically described by Anderson. If Nancy Datston was the landlady for nearly sixty years she must have been in the house before the French Revolution broke out in 1789, so that the White Ox, which has now been levelled to the ground, must have been a licensed house for something like one hundred and twenty years and possibly a great deal longer." The final two verses of his 'Murry Neet' graphically describe the scene after a night of food, song, music, dancing and general carousing. All classes had been catered for. The posher set were by the ingle, card players were in the attic, and lovers whispered their sweet nothings in another corner. The ballad ended:

But hod! I forgat - when the clock struck eleben,
The dubbler was brong in wi' wheyte bread and broon;

The White Ox Inn, the inspration for Blackell Murry Night

The gully was sharp, the girt cheese a topper,
And lumps big as lapsteanes the lads gobbled down:
Aye the douse dapper lanleady cried
'Eat and welcome,
Noo aw stepp ferret and dunnet be bleate!'
When aw were weel panged we buck'd up for blin' Jemmy,
And neest paid the shot on a girt pewter plate.

Noo full to the thropple, wi hedwarks and heartaches,
Some crap to the clock©cease a'steed of the duir;
Then sleepin and snworing teake place of their rwoaring,
And teane abuin tudder e'en laid on the fluir.
The last o' December, lang may we remember,
At five in the mworn eighteen hundred and twee:
Here's health and success to brave Johnny Dawston,

And monie sec meetings may we leeve to see."

It must have been in 1807 or early 1808 when Robert and a companion made a trip to the north-east of Scotland. His description of just one morning painted a perfect pen-picture of a ancient couple and their simple way of life.

"We arose by daylight; just as the lark quitted his dewy nest, and blithely bade Phoebus good morrow. Six Scottish miles had we to trudge without beholding house, hedge, or hazle (sic) bush. At Clatterton Shaw Toll Bar (confound all inventors of such discordant names) we beheld a miserable hovel, the smoke issuing in clouds from the door;

'It stands abuin the Water Dee,
Whar black bare hills a'roun you see;
But for a shrub, a bush, or tree,
A thousan' merks in vain ye'd gie.'

I entered, and after many a clumsy bow was paid by Joseph Walsh, an old weather©beaten cottager; he prevailed, with some difficulty, upon his guid wife, who was in bed, to rise and prepare for us anything in the shape of a breakfast.

Babby (Barbara) I never can forget. Her face was painted brown and wrinkled uncommonly by the cold hard hand of the destroyer, Time. A dirty woollen nightcap partly hid her grey hairs; but cheerfulness beamed in her countenance. Joseph had made on a blazing ingle, over which was hung a little tea-kettle, and was busily employed in sweeping the clay floor when we entered.

The sight was pleasing, nor is there aught disgraceful in the pleasing of the female sex. Hercules threw away his club and took up a spindle: and who can be so dear to man as his wife. Decency bade us to retire till poor Babby threw on her few ragged and dirty weeds; and on gazing around me fancy returned me to that place where I had spent years of bliss and years of pain." Here Robert, his memories of home stirred by his surroundings, again lapsed into poetry:

When straying on the bare-banked Dee,
Or by the mossy, streamless Cree,
Where grass plot, cottage, shrub or tree
Is seldom seen;

Eden, my thoughts oft return to you
Thy meadows green.

The thrush sings on thy fragrant bow'rs,
Spring decks thy banks with sweetest flowers,
There have I passed youth's happiest hours;
Now torn away.
Dark ruin, scowling on me, low'rs,
Where'er I stray.

A slave to pleasure I have been;
Ah! Monie changes I have seen
And oft reflection frae my e'en,
Draws the salt tears;
For thowless o'er life's busy scene,
My course I steer.

By dunces, wardlings, ay despis'd;
By lovers of the muse whyles priz'd;
I ne'er no more cou'd be advised,
(Tho' weak my lays)
To wink at Folly's whims, disguis'd,
Or vice to praise.'

Here he ended his musings, saying: "But thus might any scribbling worshipper of Apollo rhyme away, by the day, month, or year" and returned to the scene before him:

"On entering I heard Joseph gently chiding his old brown lump of love and deformity; telling her, with a good-humoured smile: 'Troph, Babby, ye are unco' like the weans, ye need muckle tayshing (teasing) this mworn!

"Much did the old creature apologise for the want of what dainties she vainly imagined we southern folk could only eat.

"The hens have no yet laid; but they were cackling around us already. She was sorry to be without white bread; being far frae mairket and carriers seldom came that way. The butter was sour and there was nae cream o' the milk. She kenn'd weel the time when she could have served us wi' a better breakfast."

"The hens, after flying on our tea-table, which Joseph had carefully propped up with peats, now kindly laid four eggs in the bed which the sonsy dame had just quitted; and these she washed well, dried with a clean napkin, and boiled in the kettle. With eggs, plenty of wholesome oatcake, country cheese, strong tea and excellent mild whisky, we made as hearty a breakfast as any couple within the purlieu of St James, for which honest Babby charged (guess, reader!) only eight pence the piece, scarcely could she be prevailed on to take more.

"Blush, ye innkeepers, who keep fawning animals preying on each guest! "Joseph Walsh was a pleasant old man, tolerably well-informed. He could talk about Washington, and America; the Galloway mountains; new intended roads; changes in his time; markets for cattle; oppressive taxes; dangerous growing power of Bonaparte, etc. etc.

"His bible, and a weekly newspaper were all he read. Happy peasant! He had been as far as Carlisle; and was surprised at the magnificence of the cathedral and the sound of its organ. O' unmusical Joseph! It resembled then the discordant noise of pigs turned loose from a mother. He was averse to the English form of worship, being a member of the Scotch church.

"A shepherd informed me that he had known better days; had kept a mill; but like too many in this wild world, had proved unfortunate. These poor children of innocence seem perfectly happy, even in this wretched hovel. Although denied many comforts of life few who inhabit the great world, sons of sloth and luxury, enjoy such content!"

Robert's talents as a writer of verse were well-known in the city but not everyone appreciated being the target of his satire.

In February, 1808, he received a threatening letter, which he revealed to the Carlisle Examiner, writing to them:

Sir, The following letter I received yesterday morning. As the production of an insect may be amusing to some readers, I wish it to be inserted in your paper. Yours, & c., R. Anderson.

The paper was delighted to use the story and printed what amounted to the death threat to Robert:
Carlisle, 15th Feb, 1808

"Sir, I understand that you are at present employing your vacant hours in composing a Song, respecting the assembly which was held at Mr Scarrows, styled the Butterfly Ball, in hopes to ridicule the characters of those who attended. I have just sent you these few lines to inform you that if it ever be the case you will have reason to repent the hour that ever you began it, for if you do suffer a publication of that description to be made public I can assure it will be the last you will publish in Carlisle or any place else, for you may depend upon it you must not expect to walk the streets of Carlisle unprotected, therefore I shall leave it to your own judgement to do what you think proper." Ironically it was signed: "A Friend"!

In 1807 Robert's beloved father died, and just one year later he left Carlisle to spend almost eleven years in Northern Ireland, first at Brookfield and later at Carnmoney. His work at Brookfield was to last only two years. The company was in trouble and Anderson was given notice to quit. He was about to leave Ireland when he received an unexpected offer of work at Carnmoney, some five mites from Belfast.

Francis Bigger, grandson of his new employer, told the tale in the Belfast Newsletter of 9.12.1926:

"On the advice of a friend he crossed over to Ireland to take service at Brookfield, near the grange of Doagh, on the Islekelly river in County Antrim. Here he worked for two years until he was employed by David Bigger, my grandfather, at the Carnmoney Cotton Printing Works where he was engaged until his employer's death in 1818. At this time the manufacture and printing of muslin and calico was a principal industry.

"During this time Anderson resided mostly with Thomas and Andrew Stewart, at Springtown in the townland of Ballyearl. He was a skilled and able workman, capable of producing excellent wood blocks for printing purposes. "During Anderson's time there was some distress which was locally relieved by charitable gatherings, when the offerings, however were sometimes exceeded by the cost of the potations. The poet took a most active part in all such efforts and would have beggared himself at any time to relieve distress." Robert Anderson would literally give his last shilling away to a worthy cause. Said Francis Bigger: "Anderson, while resident at Carnmoney, almost rivalled Goldsmith in his charity; sparing himself nothing. He would have given all his food or even his very clothes to those who were in need."

There was a drawback to his charitable work. Alcohol. So much charity by Robert led to another kindness returned. Said Francis Bigger: "He fell a victim to inebriety, a habit which forever afterwards followed him, shadowing him to the grave."

Robert recalled: "Charity Balls, as they are termed, were frequently held, and at these I collected considerable sums, and, without doubt, saved numbers from the grave. Subscriptions were liberally attended to at the Print Works, whenever they were deemed necessary, not only for the wretched families employed there, but for the helpless throughout the neighbourhood. On these occasions I was uniformly appointed collector and I still pray for the happiness of my fellow workman."

Robert was staying at an old farmhouse, Springtown, near Ballyearl, with brothers Thomas and Andrew Stewart, together with a number of women, and it was at this time that he wrote many verses, most of them appearing in the Belfast Newsletter and the Commercial Chronicle, as well as in a collection of poems published in Belfast in 1810 by Alexander Mackey." It gave him the entree to the literary elite of Belfast. He was friendly with other local muses such as Andrew Mackenzie, the Bard of Dunover, and Samuel Thomson, from Templepatrick, who could boast of having spent a night at the house of Rabbie Burns. Robert had made the pilgrimage too, but was only privileged to sit in the poet's chair and talk to his widow.

But Robert Anderson did not devote all of his time to charity work and the writing of verse. Ever ready with a silver tongue, and a silver pen, the ladies' man may have given a clue to amorous adventures when he confessed: "During the many years I spent in the Emerald Isle, I must plead guilty to many irregularities of conduct which often ended in misery."

Was he referring to the almost continuous correspondence between himself and the mysterious "Mrs M", who he also addressed as "Maria", "Marianne", or Mrs Moline?

Certainly he seemed to be excessive in his endearments and compliments to the lady.

What must have been one of the first of his letters was formal in address, but nevertheless written in true dramatic style. It was post-dated

120

Brookfield,
October 18th, 1808:
Dear Madam!
The night was dark, and wet, and windy, and the ways were knee-deep in mire when last I left your cottage, but far would I wander reckless of the bitterest storm Boreas ever conjured up in the frigid north, and even:
"Laugh at the tempest of the night,
Tho' not one star shot forth its light."
To enjoy such a feast as your company affords.

The evening was spent in that happy manner, on which the mind reflects with many an agreeable sensation. Alas! How different was my employment the following night; seated among ignoramuses, fretting over a few shillings at an insipid but noisy card party. I hate gaming, and thought more of you. The night we parted, 'ere the clock in my humble cabin had drowsily rung the second hour, I had read the first volume of your strange, witty, delightful and well-written Romance. A second perusal has afforded me pleasure, infinitely heightened, which is seldom the case, dear Madam. The typographical errors are numerous, and not unfrequently ridiculous; and pardon me for saying, the punctuation has not been properly attended to. The paper and half-binding are equally a disgrace to the town of Belfast.

Of the plot of your work I am ignorant, conjecture being yet only just awakened, which is rarely the case indeed, for we commonly have the catastrophe in view; on reading a first volume.

I will not flatter you, Mrs Moline; but truth, sacred truth makes me declare, many of your sketches possess the wild grandeur and sublimity of imagination, which have been so much the admiration of the public, from the pencils of Salvatore Rosa, or Michael Angelo (sic) while some of your scenes have all the rich tenderness and bewitching colouring of a Guido. You have justly made two of the greatest writers your models; Le Sage and Mrs Radcliffe. Like theirs, your characters are strongly marked. Adela is lovely; and yet there seems no labour in the ingenious authoress, to make her so perfect. This is a great beauty in the department of literature you have chosen. Your language and sentiment are such as we expect from an experienced writer, who has not only waded through a mass of literature, but studied deeply the human heart; and your incident, (which is remarkable of a writer in her sixteenth year) is neither tediously introduced, or mawkishly lugged in by the head and shoulders. Go on, ingenious and fair authoress! Accept the tribute of a humble rhymester, little-known by the world and still less favoured by Fortune.

May you be prosperous in the literary vineyard, and Fame record your name with her favourite daughters, is my sincere wish. If unfortunate repine not, remember what has so oft been the fate of genius. Favour me with the three volumes of your Romance; and with them the elegant poem from your pen, which, with which I am much delighted. Romney Robinson's poems, and Poems by Mrs Ledbeater (lately Miss Shackleton) I have just read; and will send you the latter, but you will not derive much pleasure from the perusal. She displays a goodness of heart, more than a poetical talent.

I propose doing myself the honour of visiting you on Sunday, provided you will not think me an intruder; one of the many characters to me extremely detestable. Perhaps you on that day will be engaged with society more agreeable; or you mean to devote it to study; if so, may the Muse be favourable,

Name, by the boy, when I must expect to see you. Accept the trifling effusions you were pleased to praise. I wish they had been more deserving the approbation of so sensible a lady.

Here Robert ends his letter in the most formal of styles, signing off with "My respects to your mother, and, believe me, dear Madam, Your obliged and obedient servant Robt Anderson."

Some two weeks later a short note, still in formal style, read: "R. Anderson presents his respectful compliments to Mrs M and hopes that all are well and happy around the cottage fireside. An unavoidable engagement to the theatre prevents his calling with the books; and is sorry an intended journey to morrow will deprive him of the interesting conversation he has listened to with delight when in company of the fair authoress of 'The Cottage of the Appenines'. Will do himself the pleasure of visiting her the very first opportunity!
Brookfield, Oct 30th, 1808.

Nineteen days was to pass before he wrote again. This time it was very much more than a note; to say the least it was a long-winded, philosophical dissertation that could have been used as the basis of many a

vicar's sermon!
Belfast, West Street, November 18th, 1808.
Dear Mrs M,
How oft it happens that when the heart pants for the enjoyment of any particular person's company, some evil genius smites us poor half hunted mortals, and we are, or seem to be, pestered with all the devilish ills that are aggravating. Thus has it fared with me. Believing myself a welcome guest at the Cottage of Literature I would not so long have been an absentee; had not lameness prevented me the pleasure of making a visit. God's will be done! An inflammation in my left foot makes me a cripple; but rather would I continue so than be compelled to sit on thorns submitting to the cold unsocial formalities and stupefying customs so frequently witnessed by any common observer at half polite and heterogeneous mock-fashionable parties. Had my sight, or right hand been affected, either would have called forth many a bitter complaint; but while I can see to peruse the works of the eiightened and immortal few - have power to wield my pen in defence of virtue - to correspond with one individual so possessed of your extraordinary talents and comprehensive mind, I will proudly scorn the pains and afflictions puny mortals are doomed to bear and laugh at the freaks of fickle Fortune.
Here Robert lapsed into one of his instant rhyming moods:
Fortune and Rab hae always liv'd at strife,
I court her not; she frowns indignant still:
And since uncertain is the play of life,
I swear whae'er my lot, scorn her I will,
For let the goodless kick the ba'
Or let the gypsy smile,
Her frowns to me are naught at a',
Her joys sae oft beguile.
Pardon an egotistic trifle, dear Madam! I am scribbling without aim like a ship at sea without a rudder. There is a happy knack of combining sentiment, description, and the variety of commonplace chit-chat, in epistolary writing where it is necessary, yet must be concealed; this I have ardently admired in many, particularly you Madam, but could never attain it. How have you spent time since I last saw you? An impudent question! methinks you will exclaim; for time with you is spent in the noblest and best

of purposes, that of adding to the happiness of fellow creatures; by boldly encountering vulgar prejudices; and instructing a numerous body of speaking, but unthinking, animals who have too long been kept in darkness. A few days will, I hope in God, will enable me to crawl up to the Retreat of the Muses; for wherever Fate may throw me during the short pilgrimage of life, the indescribable pleasures enjoyed in your company will be dearly cherished. There seems to exist a pleasing congeniality of sentiment between us. O' that the world could, with propriety, flatter me with a similarity of genius! Since closing the last sentence a sonnet has taken possession of my brainless head. You shall have it, with all its weaknesses, but be indulgent to the puny child. My next may be better. So trifling a production, on so fair and intelligent a being, a Sun among my rushlights, compared with her sex around us, ought not to be submitted to to the inspection of vulgar eyes.

Then follows the sonnet - inscribed to Mrs Moline, authoress of The Cottage of the Appenines:

"Daughter of Genius, sweet it is to me,
Where poorer slaves must bow to wretched proud,
Thy cot to seek; and hear thy converse free,
In praise of virtuous freedom justly loud;
Next argue for thy sex, oft basely bowed,
By tyrant man; to keenest misery.
Daughter of Truth; this heart-felt wish I send,
May sorrow ne'er with night-shade strew thy way,
But Health, and Hope, and Peace thy steps attend,
And long the Muses o'er their favourite bend,
Prompting the legend strong, or sprightly lay!
Weak flows my verse; yet will I proud commend
A learn'd Instructress, and fair virtuous friend.

If your patience be not entirely exhausted, you are, indeed, Madam, a blessed woman. Burn this, I beseech you, fair reader. I will see you at the hour appointed, I mean write, at or before that time.

Adieu - God bless you! R. Anderson"

He was still unable to get out and about when he penned the next letter to Maria:

"This devilish ill-natured looking foot of mine gets worse every hour.

Administer comfort to the wretched, dear Maria, for you are good and know everything. I am nailed to the chimney corner, quite a fixture; like a rap to a counter. The promised visit of today must be deferred, and it makes me peevish as an old maid after being ninety-nine times jilted. Now poulticing, plastering, fomenting, washing, groaning at the advice of every fool! I am debarred the pleasure of seeing your sweet face; but can I not obtain a sight of your pretty Tale? How would a long©faced gummy lump of hypocrisy, a prudish moral-monger, start on hearing such a question, Marianne! After deliberate reflection, forgotten (if possible) in the fair writer, a valued friend, you shall have my candid opinion. Be not disheartened good Mrs, if the sapient jousts of editors, the squinting, grave©looking diffusers of knowledge to some who can, to others who cannot, read, reject your studies! Keep in mind that immortal but most unfortunate boy, Chatterton. Oft, in fancy, I see him wandering from friends and dear home, to the great overgrown mart of human genius. Now buoyed up by expectations, naturally the result of so vast, so independent, a mind. Now fondly cherishing the hope of supporting an aged mother and a feeble sister. Now spurned by the venal traffickers of literature. Now driven ... no more of the gloomy picture! Poor boy! Rich in thy unfeeling Country's love! Let us thank God, Maria, for the gift of a feeling heart, and a tear to shed for ill©fated genius, on the unfortunate of very description! You accuse me of flattery unjustly in your letter.

"Say, what advantage may I hope from thee,
Who no revenue hast, save thy good name
To feed and clothe thee?"

Who knows better than you, Madam, how to distinguish between the heart-felt tribute, due to merit; and the obsequious fawnings of a coxcomb? The last are commonly offered the impenetrable dullness, or bloated folly, wallowing amidst wealth. "Truth ought to pass free as the air we breathe," said King Stanislaus. Let it be the general currency of the sensible part of the world; then will the enlightened be as one great family.

Thanks, madam, for your poetical morceau addressed to myself. The subject was unworthy your Muse; but the lines are beautiful. Talk of flattery! I may justly retaliate! 'Tis no more than listening to what we wish were truth; and oft, in fact, believe. There is a passage or two in your poem, not perfectly clear to my clouded understanding; but we behold spots on the orb of day. I compared it with mine, addressed to you the night before. Psha! 'Ere had I well commenced, reason had declared strongly in your favour. A reader of sense would glance over my trifles, and with a yawn of cold indifference announce them "tolerably smooth!" He turns to yours, and exclaims enthusiastically "These are the wild flights of an enlightened understanding. This writer evinces extraordinary proofs of poetical genius!"

Such, Marianne, will be the verdict, given at no distant day, by the lofty bench of critics. Your language and mode of thinking of that great English Collossus of learning, Doctor Johnson. Long may you wield his Herculean club; and brandish it, a terror to folly, but a blessing to ignorance! A comparison may settle the point in question. How daringly the bird of Jove, conscious of its own strength, at pleasures above this nether world, heedless of this crazy race who inhabit it. Again, mark the Linnet, the eagle-like how gladly would it fly: but on making the attempt to soar it it falls. The eagle you; the half fledg'd linnet I!

Congreve observes:

"All we ought, or can, in this dark state,Is what we have admir'd to imitate."

What a ludicrous figure would Giles the clown cut, in offering to an audience one of Handel's concertos on the violin; when he had been only accustomed to play 'God save the King' and the 'Rogues' March. Even so contemptible would I appear by aiming at anything higher than simple Ballad, or light composition.

Do, my dear good creature, favour me by the boy, with any book that might beguile a few hours:for I could even read the surprising history of "Jack the Giantkiller," or the marvellous exploits of "Robin Hood and Little John."

Send me not any historical memoir of the powerful potentates of the present day; for they are a pack of white slave merchants and licenced murderers of thoughtless multitudes: their hellish deeds are too severely felt. Perhaps you have something in the pleasing walk of poetry that to me may be new. I expect not anything from your pen; to request a glance at the sacred scraps of your study amounts to presumption. This is not accordant with the customs of literature.

You ask me 'how time passes?' You have seen a spider quite exhausted. I draw a little, and flute little, and groan a little, and doctor a little, and eat a little, and talk a little, and read a little, and study a little, and scribble a little, and sleep a little; thus pass the hours away.

Best, and most sensible of woman, Adieu! Robt Anderson, West Street, Nov 6th, 1808.

It is obvious from Robert's letters that Maria was a very sick person, although there are no clues to the illness from which she suffered. Robert was ever anxious, and kept a keen eye on her condition. The next letter could have been a presage of her early death.

Brookfield, six in the morning.

"Dearest of women,

I trust in God you are recovered from that illness under which you endured such anguish at our friend's last night. The sight was truly distressing; I would gladly have suffered more than Maria, could it have alleviated what the best of creatures laboured under. Oh! Heavens! The cause © Pardon me, dear Maria! I would not awaken a painful idea in such a mind, or occasion that tender bosom a pang, on any consideration. No-one living can ever feel a greater anxiety to promote another's happiness than I do yours. Woe unto him or her who thinks otherwise!"

Then follows yet another poem wishing her well and he ends with "Adieu Dear Maria, R. Anderson.

His next letter referred to his boyhood days of poverty and a contained a strange remark which would indicate that Maria had accused him of being hard-hearted. Had he shied away from becoming more deeply involved with her? Or had he just failed to show concern over her suffering?

Brookfield, Monday morning.

Dear Marianne,

Sick at heart and trembling like one in a fit of the ague, since Friday evening I have scarcely been able to hold up my head; and with the greatest difficulty have crawled here. Why, Maria, do you harshly accuse me of hard-heartedness? The truth is my feelings have frequently led me to the brink of ruin; but wherever Fate may throw me, when I cease to feel for your bodily or mental sufferings, may I cease to exist.

From my birth I have been inured to distress:
"For Poverty,
My parents, kindred, all, still kept in bondage,

And at my birth presided. Luckless hour,
That gave me to the world!"

I am thankful for being blessed with fortitude which enables me to smile at poverty, or the scorn of mankind. Oft has an anxiety to promote the welfare of ungrateful fellow creatures, made me too forgetful, alas! of my own interests. Pardon me, dear madam, your letter provoked me to this silly strain of egotism. May you never again be pestered with what is so unworthy your notice!

Your request cannot be complied with (impute this also to a hardness of heart) Early yesterday morning I was applied to, in bed, to lend a sum of money to a worthy man at this place; who has a small family and a sick, helpless wife. To those who know me best, I appeal whether my purse is ever shut against such wretchedness? What little I had left was lent to the good woman where I lodge, whose husband was disappointed in receiving his monthly pay. The bearer (of the letter) knows there is not a cutter or Printer here but is deeply indebted to me; I may include others about the place, and consider the whole as lost. Is this, too, hard-heartedness? Players are too often a heavy tax upon such of their friends as possess a generous heart; and if I mistake not, you are deluded by Mrs _____. She grieves, forsooth, like a child because she cannot dress in a manner their slender income ill entities her too! I wish she may never have greater cause to repine.

It is this system of extravagance, in dress and mockery of high life, which involves in perpetual distress thousands of that wretched profession. Mark me, Madam; the lady above-mentioned will, while she lives, be one of that unfortunate number!

Every exertion shall be used by me for their benefit, more they have no right to expect.

I introduced you to Mrs____; but such is the openness of your nature that it is a duty incumbent upon me to caution you against associating with any of the profession. My feeling heart prompted me to give this advice with the same affection I would to a wife, sister or daughter. You may think this rudeness. Experience will whisper you otherwise.

So great is my wish to be the promoter of your happiness, had a similar request been made for yourself, I call God to witness how eagerly I would have flown to every friend, rather than the best, and to me the dearest of her sex should have suffered. No more on the subject."

Here Robert returns more pleasant and happier subjects:

"I have transcribed your Songs, with some alterations, but am afraid our ideas will not coincide. 'The Maniac' I decline meddling with, from what passed on my last visit. The whole, with some others for your amusement, are at your service.

On maturely weighing the contents of this (written when the mind is deeply depressed; and bowed down by sickness) if you then think me unfeeling, or culpable, I beseech you, Maria, think me no longer worthy your friendship. Adieu!

Yours affectionately,
Robt. Anderson.

On March 25, 1809, just one year after his arrival, he opened up his heart. The letter he was answering must have indicated some deeper feelings by Maria, and she had obviously instructed him not to open it before reaching home. Was it a love letter?

"Dear Marianne,

And, I will add, best of thy sex! That letter, more to me than pen can describe, remained unopened until I reached my lodging; according to agreement. It was to me like succouring to the starving pilgrim; or rain sent from heaven to a parched sufferer.

Why do you apologise for so tender a proof of esteem? Why, dear Madam, blame yourself for impertinent curiosity? O, Maria! I have perused it attentively; and bathed it with a tear of gratitude for such unmerited attention. It convinces me there is one whose sensibility and feeling heart makes her dear to me as the redcurrant which warms this sickly frame; and little reason had I to suppose such a mortal would ever express a wish to lessen my sorrows by sharing them. Twelve months have flown on rapid wing, this day, this very hour, since my arrival in Belfast. I dreamt not of meeting one of your extraordinary powers of mind; but bless the hour which threw us together. 0' that I could recline my head, my weary head upon your bosom, Marianne, and utter to you what gives to many a sorrow birth! It must not, cannot be! Heed me not! I love you, for your goodness, and will ever pray for your happiness. I sigh for your sorrows; but will save you the pain of ever knowing mine. Compare me to a broken reed, Maria, it soon withers;

and the traveller knoweth not where it grew. No more on this, except the following simple effusion of the moment. We cannot think such trifles are poetry. Self deprecating? Certainly Robert laid it on a bit thick when he wrote:: "A secret pang oft rends my breast,
Soft Pity's tear could not remove;
It robs me of night's soothing rest,
And days of pain it makes me prove.
It made me soon a child of care,
And stole from me Health's roseate bloom;
But I this pang must silent bear,
And hope for peace in the dark tomb."
Surely a little melodramatic. A death wish! Peace in the tomb!! Robert, who delighted so much in life!

He continued:

"Accept the following sonnet, if fourteen such lines may be so called; and pardon a poor rhyming sinner for so abruptly closing an epistle to an adminstering angel.

Accept the warmest wishes of this grateful heart; and o' believe it Susceptible to every tender tie,
Of friendship's solid flame, or love's soft sigh.
Sonnet to Maria. You ask, Maria, why I droop my head,
And why thus let dejection cloud my brow? Alas! Life's various prospects all are fled, Which frolic Fancy once before me spread, And naught but misery waits me now; For long a captive by false pleasures led,
And madd'ning Mirth, th' unheeded minutes flew' While projects vain were idly nourished.

Lost, too, are friends who vow'd eternal truth; Yes, friendship's balm drives heavy cares away! But little dreams poor unsuspecting youth, Misfortunes makes e'en friendship soon decay! O wonder not, Maria, if my breast Now harbors Sorrow, life©consuming guest!

Adieu, dearest woman! Robt Anderson.
Sunday morning.

PS: I am disappointed in seeing you today; but if it be not inconvenient to you, Madam, I will visit the cottage tomorrow evening. My wish is that you be better engaged. Write by the boy (they evidently used a

130

courier to pass their letters back and forth)

Afford me the pleasure of reading you are well and happy. God bless you, Maria!

R.A.

Some two weeks later he was again writing from West Street, but after the protestations of love and affection of his previous letter seemed to commence in terse manner. However he was soon back in flattering mood when describing his planned move to a new home:

"Have the goodness to return the "School For Authors" to Mr M soon as possible, dearest Madam; but beware of endangering your happiness in the next world by glancing over a Play on this day of holy work. 0' prejudice! Accursed vile prejudice! How weak is man to be kept thy slave; when by a feeble effort he may break thy chain!

Having being attempting to stammer on Parnassian stilts, or in plain language, cursed with the itch of scribbling since six this morning, this ought have commenced with

The low'ring clouds obscure the placid sky,

Spring o'er the earth a charming sorrow throws;

But such pompous gossamery nonsense, however grateful to the ear of a tasteless, novel-reading ignoramus, would be disgusting to the fair authoress of 'Rosa'.

I wish to inform you (who, I flatter myself, am interested in my welfare, a bargain was this morning nearly sealed for me to lodge near Brookfield in future.

The cottage is an humble one. So am I! Grandeur would but ill bow the head to enter it. With such I have naught to do! No garden adorns its front, nor does the woodbine, jasmine, wild rose or laburnum vie with each other in creeping up its porch, for porch it has none. Yet it contains a little parlor, the quintessence or retired snugness; where I may sometimes muse in peace, thinking of the few dearest to my heart. What makes me prize it most is, by straying six paces to the right, or to my left, I can cast mine eye across the vale, and imagine I see you near the `Muses' Bower'. Lend me your 'Yorick's Letters.' They shall be carefully returned. My good wishes to your dear mother and Mr and Mrs A. Tell him I mean, god willing, `ere my head is pillowed, to transcribe for him a hymn which cannot fail pleasing one of his liberal mind, and sound understanding.

Peace be within the walls of your cottage; and happiness to all such as are worthy of becoming its inmates is the fervent wish of -

Robt Anderson.

On one occasion we find, for once, Robert writing to a man, a Mr A - of Belfast, discussing the work, and life, of another writer, declaring: "I have not anywhere, my dear friend, read a better production than the enclosed; nor is there one living for whom I would sooner transcribe a copy. Preserve me from the company of the wretch, were he even the proud possessor of millions, who could read it without shedding a tributary tear to the memory of Britain's greatest statesman, the friend of the poor African, the 'man of the people!'

"It was written by Captain Morris; an ingenious writer, but a wicked wit, too like Rochester or Burns. Like them, he was of an open cheerful temper, and fond of the misnomer'd joys of the bottle. He sunk into the lowest scenes of intoxicated dissipation; frequently satirising his best friends (like poor Burns) merely to gratify ignorance or folly. The splendid talents Rochester and Burns possessed, not being guided by Virtue, soon hastened their ruin. "Each sent into the world what better have been destroyed, repenting when it was too late. Genius is too often led astray by the false glitter of fame; scorning the real path to her temple; but every man of sense must soberly confess a well-spent life is the only promoter of health, and this foundation of earthly happiness. Morris is living; but has for many years been dead to the literary world, having long laboured under mental derangement."

This unknown correspondent was obviously part of the literary circle that met at the home of Maria, Robert's letter continued: "Doubtless you would visit 'The Cottage of the Muses' today. I hope you passed a social afternoon, as usual, and pleasure reigned in the midst of instruction and well-timed debate. For me, God knows, I hate your tame, upright, and accommodating yes and no animals, even when decked out in the tinsel trappings of wealth; and would sooner sit alongside blunt honesty in tatters. I felt a strong desire to have made one of the happy group this evening, but thought proper to drink tea t my lodgings. It will be the last Sunday of my remaining here. We are loth to part, but I will be happier out of town; having it in my power to avoid idle temptations, which here beset me in different shapes. The hand of a friend will be even dearer than ever; and believe me, dear sir, there are none whose esteem I court more than yours and your amiable lady. To her present my respects.

That you may long be the happy possessors of every sorrow-soothing balm is the wish of your obliged friend,

Robert Anderson.

His next letter reveals his dismay at not meeting Maria when he had expected to do so, and a mysterious warning:

"At the appointed hour last night I waited on our friends, Mrs and Mrs ____ ; but you were fled Maria, as from the pursuit of an enemy. Your reason I cannot guess.

Avoid all connection with ____ who pretends to feel anxious about purchasing your Works. He is ... Madam, I will not say what he is; but feel a pride in cautioning you against all such. You are sensible enough to quiz all like him; but alas! You are too credulous!

I am to drink tea with our friends, Mr and Mrs D this evening. I wish you would endeavour to make one of the party; for trust me, Marianne, 'You are dear to me,

As the light to the e'e!'

Am I ever again to be blessed with your company? If so, say when and where. If not, give a reason.

Favour me with Sterne's "Letters to Eliza". They are for a young lady's perusal, with whom you would be delighted.

God knows, in these days of frippery, there are few worth the notice of Mrs M___ ; but while I am considered one of the happy number, let me be thankful, and pray for one so dear.

Yours affectionately,

Robt Anderson

Frustration seemed to follow frustration. Having missed seeing Maria when she had "fled as though from the pursuit of an enemy" he then appears to have agreed to partner her to the theatre, where Richard Kemble was appearing, but then has to cancel the appointment because of an immediate publishing deadline:

"I could not, dearest Maria, attend the theatre last night, had it even been to have accompanied and angel instead of the best of female mortals. Writing for ___ what was absolutely to be printed this morning, engaged me during the evening. Great was the disappointment. My thoughts wandered so from the subject, I have frequently liked to have written Marianne instead of John or Thomas. Be pleased to admit the above as an apology; for I bow to you, good madam, as a child ought unto its mother. To a mind comprehensive as yours, the tragic powers of Kemble would afford infinite delight. Few among the million who attend theatrical representations are so capable of appreciating just talent, and I hope you were gratified with the celebrated actor.

"Tis six, and a fine gray morning, without dew. O' that you were employed with the pen at this hour, dearest of women,,, or tracing the banks of the Logan with rosy health! Suppose we were seated in your little dell, piping an hour away? Or engaged in interesting converse, while enraptur'd with the varied beauties of Nature, which never cloy the mind of sensibility. Could anything be more pure, more innocent? Alas!, dear Maria, what a vile world we inhabit, that will not even allow the delights sacred to Virtue!"

Was it that the etiquette of the day demanded that a married woman could not be alone with a single man? Then Robert returns to his hopes.

"Possibly I may be blest with your smile this evening at the cottage. If not you will share my heart's prayers e're my head be pillowed.

Forget not a line to our brother Gaelus (Poet Andrew McKenzie, the Bard of Dunover) Court not your Muse for the departed infant of every fool; nonsense like the following is applicable to poor blubbering Bobby M___ . Says an old Jackdaw `O-hoh! O-hoh!

I'm robbed of my greatest pride!!!'says the young Jackdaw, `D`d true, Pappa!

I lik'd not this world, so I died!!!'

The stanzas on visiting my mother's grave were never shewn. They may afford pleasure to a mind like yours, dear Marianne, fraught with sensibility. I care not for the multitude. The tenderness will make up for want of poetical flights. O' return it carefully, that I may sometimes wet it with a tear; for no effusion of a brainless scribbler ever came more warm from a feeling heart. Write and say you are well.

Adieu, Maria,
Yours with affection, R. Anderson

It overjoys me dearest Marianne, to read your notes and think of the pleasure your company will afford me at the theatre tomorrow evening. Rest assured, I will meet you at the time and place appointed; and seated by you I could not possibly envy, or even notice, the grandeur around us. My respectful compliments to Mr and Mrs M. I would have called, and seen you home; but am expecting Mr Turnbull every moment. Heaven bless you! And blessed must all be who are like Maria,
Yours truly Robt Anderson.

What turned out to be the penultimate letter amongst Robert Anderson's papers again poses a question. Just what did Maria say to Robert that robbed him of a night's sleep, and according to him, many more to come?

My dearest Madam,
The boy cannot wait; consequently I have just time to ask how you are this morning. I cannot enjoy the pleasure of seeing you today; but tomorrow I may call with a friend.

'Maria! Your mysterious conversation has cost me a night's rest, and will cost m many; but heaven knows, I would lose a thousand for your sake. Peace to your bosom!

Affectionately adieu! Robt Anderson

The last of the letters to be found among the Anderson papers was a lengthy one. It came as the Brookfield work ended and he was facing a possible return to Cumberland.

Dear Mrs M _,
A wish to visit the cottage is what I anxiously feel, but I wish in vain. On Monday morning I arose nearly deprived of hearing; and remain so at this moment. Sometimes the confused soundings in my head resemble the noise of a frightful cataract; even the falls of Niagara. At present it seems as if a hundred Highlanders were stunning me, each with a large discordant bagpipe. Had I been, unfortunately, a devoted victim to a scolding wife, or a foolish one, which is worse, deafness might indeed have been a welcome relief: but alas! Maria, the society of the few, the very few t court must be relinquished, unless an unexpected change takes place. Who can sit, observing the motion of lips, when his ear refuses to drink the sound?

No more I hear the neighbr'ng bell,
Than if it toll'd my funeral knell.

I will turn to another subject, even more painful. Since I enjoyed the pleasure of seeing you, dear madam, one of my employers informed me my services at Brookfield may be dispensed with in a few days. Yes, a few days will find me a helpless, heartbroken, exil'd wretch; wandering in vain for bread, and no friendly smile to soothe distress. When we become reduced to the extremity of calamity, and cherished hopes are all fled, then 'friendship wears another garb' and what had the appearance of open sincerity is transformed into cold disdain, or the scowl of abhorrence."

Once again Robert was inspired to poetry:

O Maria! How sweet it is, if,
When oppress'd by want and sorrow,
Life's a painful load to bear,
We, by friendship's magic, borrow,
Hours of bliss, and smile at care!
By whatever ills surrounded,
That can cheer the gloomy way;
But without it, self confound'd,
Life's a joyless winter's day.

My situation has for some time been an unpleasant one; for "'tis hard to sit in Rome and fight with the Pope", but to use an old proverb

'A happin, a herrin, and a bawbee,
Is gear enough for folks like me.'

He is wise, Maria, who is timely wary; and foolish is he who forgets himself: for 'it is better to be envied than pitied.' This sting of poverty makes many a man everyone's dog who chooses to whistle; and that I acknowledge with many a sigh.

Little did I think that this would come to pass when the proud vessel bore me thru the white-topp'd billows to Erin's happy isle. Light beat my heart, as that of a playful infant, for Hope, my smiling companion, pointed to a fair prospect. Alas! The deceiver is fled, and it has vanished from my view."

Eventually his cries of woe and poetical breast-beating are put to one side, and once again, as ever, is solicitous, continuing his letter:

"I long to hear how you are, dear madam. God knows you have your share of bodily and mental suffering. Your cup is full, Marianne. If you

136

should be unable to drop me a line; say by the bearer you are better and I will rejoice. Did you enjoy the wish'd for pleasure in town on Monday? My prayers were at that hour for your happiness; and I caution you to be careful of your health."

Then, once more, Robert teases those who would know more about the relationship with Maria, revealing:

"I have many things to communicate, but dare not commit such thoughts to paper; and lament deafness the more, because I may exclaim 'a little while, and ye see me not!' Have you heard of Gaelus' health since Mr D's return? I flatter myself with the hope of an excursion to Dunover, to use the cold, detested word, farewell, to our favourite bard."

Here Robert's copies of the letters come to sudden end, the remaining pages of his pocket book stay tantalisingly blank. We must ever wonder about his relationship with Maria for there were to be no more privileged peeps into his personal life.

So who was Maria, alias Marianne, alias Mrs M, alias Mrs Moline, the woman he praised in such an effusive manner?

In later years the mystery deepened. Among a selection of songs ands poems he dedicated to Mrs Howard of Corby Castle was a sonnet to Maria. He supplied Mrs Howard with a footnote in which he called Maria Mrs Munster! The footnote read: "The late Mrs Munster of Belfast. She has long been known as an authoress and chose that signature in Magazines, Newspapers, etc. She commenced her literary career in early youth by publishing 'The Cottage of the Appenines, a Romance in four volumes. This work, which was completed in her sixteenth year proves her to be a warm admirer of the celebrated Mrs Radcliffe. In 'Rosa' a tale, she has displayed a knowledge of the world in a story replete with interesting incident. Her language and pathos cannot fail to please the lovers of Sterne, or the author of the 'Man of Feeling' - altho' she may truly assert with Cameron's

"My cradle was the couch of care,
And sorrows rocked me in it."

Yet no one bore the crosses of life with greater fortitude nor did cheerfulness forsake her when the tomb seemed yawning for her reception. Sensibility, vivacity, and a philanthropic spirit could not fail to make Maria the admiration of many a learned and respectable circle. She died in January

1819.

To her this author is indebted for much useful information and whether the path of life he has to pursue be spread with flowers or scattered with thorns he will pray for Maria of the Cottage."

The footnote revealed that Robert knew that Maria was seriously ill. She was just twenty-nine years old when she died.

Did they have a love affair? Maria did send him a poem which could be open to interpretation.

It was headed "Lines, by Mrs Moline." It read:

> *O' thou who knowest life's busy scene,*
> *Hast felt its hopes, each care and joy;*
> *Say, does it still bring anguish keen?*
> *Must falsehood ever truth annoy?*
>
> *If I repose on friendship's breast,*
> *Must I still meet the rankling thorn?*
> *Or if to love, I fly for rest,*
> *Must this warm heart still suffer scorn?*
>
> *If touch'd by genius' vivid fire,*
> *Must I the finest feelings lose?*
> *And seem to see, to feel, admire,*
> *But as the hacknied world must choose?*
>
> *Oh! Tell me quick! And I' believe,*
> *That Fancy paints the view thus drear;*
> *Oh! Say that I myself deceive,*
> *And bid me hope, and cease to fear!*
>
> *But if my pencil draws too true,*
> *Then let me live, and die unknown;*
> *Nor eager paint a world to view,*
> *Where flow'rs are few, but thorns thick sown!*

Robert at one time wrote her an epigram headed 'On a Lady's Disposition':

"Maria pines, the Muses drop a tear;
The Loves and Graces watch her with a sigh;
The envious of her sex e'en sad appear,
Then o' how few with such a face can vie!"

Was it just possible that Maria truly loved him, yet received only scorn and thistles? But in another notebook of miscellaneous writings Robert wrote five stanzas headed "On receiving a present from one long and truly esteemed.

Yes, on it I will gaze and sigh,
And next my heart the prize will wear;
Ev'n Death's keen terrors I'd defy,
'Ere man from me the Gift shou'd tear!

An exile tho' I'm doom'd to stray;
Where'er my vagrant feet may rove,
I'll kiss it, with a tear, and say,
O' had it been the gift of love!
But love, alas! Has brought me low,
And none from ruin can me save;
'Tis mine to bear a load of woe,
Till Sorrow sinks me in the grave.

Ah! Precious gift! On which I gaze,
May thy late owner ne'er endure
The pang that on this bosom prays,
The pain she proudly scorn'd to cure!

If e'er she deign to think of me
May no rude cares disturb her breast!
For her my daily pray'r shall be,
The fair destroyer of my rest!

Were these verses dedicated to Maria? Or were there others who had scorned him? But again the mystery deepens.

The British Library catalogues Maria's book: The Cottage of the Appenines, or the Castle of Novina. A romance. The name of the authoress? Marianne Kenley!

Early in 1817 a rumour that Robert Anderson was dead, was circulating in the city. The Carlisle Patriot added credence to the tale, printing: "It is much to be feared that Mr Anderson, the ingenious author of the Cumberland Ballads, etc., has met with a watery grave. He embarked at Belfast, about seven weeks ago, in the company of one Robert Peat, a native of this part of the country, and several others, on board the Catharine of Maryport, which vessel has not been heard of. What tends more strongly to confirm the loss of the vessel is the fact that the broken boat of the Catharine was lately washed on shore at the mouth of Maryport harbour."

Not so! The following edition of the paper carried a letter from one of Robert's friends, named Turnbull, saying there was no truth in the report. He had taken no passage in any vessel sailing for Cumberland, nor did he have any intention of doing so, and that he never was in better health and spirits than at that time!

Two years later Anderson DID return from Ireland, in the Spring of 1819, to find waiting for him something of a hero's welcome! He recalled: "Few persons, on returning to the place of their nativity, have experienced more kindness; not only from my former companions but also from many that were unknown to me previously, both rich and poor. A Public dinner was given, in honour of my return, at Mr Gibson's, of the Grey Goat, at which a numerous and respectable party attended under the able presidency of Mr Henry Pearson, solicitor, whose humour has amused all classes of his fellow citizens; and the evening was spent in a manner highly flattering to the humble individual it was intended to honour."

The Reverend Thomas Ellwood gave the decline of Calico printing in Belfast as the reason for his return, and said: "He had every reason to be gratified with the reception which he received from all classes amongst those to whom his works had made him known, and he was shortly after advised to publish his works in order to make some provision for his declining years." Robert reluctantly agreed, but only because some sort of income was necessary, saying: "Diffidence would have prevented me from making such an attempt had not necessity forced me to do it. A committee was appointed who have used every exertion to ensure my happiness in the winter of life and the same anxiety has been shown by many in various parts of the Kingdom." The Reverend Ellwood continued: "Two volumes were accordingly published at Carlisle in 1820; prefixed by 'An Essay on the character and manners of the Peasantry Of Cumberland' from the pen of his friend Thomas Sanderson; and a memoir written by himself.

"The issue of this edition, notwithstanding the long and most influential list of subscribers by which it is headed does not seem to have brought him that needful aid that was expected, there is no certain evidence of what he did or what he did not receive from the various edition of his works..."

The list of subscribers was indeed an influential one; included were the names of William Wordsworth and fellow lakes poet Robert Southey!

Robert was to spend the rest of his life in Carlisle, and in 1820 was soon again out and about in his beloved county. He rejoiced in the countryside and all it had to offer and had many a tale to enliven the chronicles of his wandering. On a long ramble through the north of the county he found himself fascinated by the Spa, its history, and the characters who came to take the water at Gilsland.

"Along the dry bed of the River King, where tree, bush and shrub is seldom seen; and after frequent rests and refreshing pulls from a bottle of whisky and water, in crossing the high tract called Spadeadam Waste, we arrived at Gilsland between nine and ten o'clock.

"This spot, of late years, became a fashionable resort, so little described, and by many perhaps deemed unworthy a description, can nevertheless boast of romantic scenery: Here stupendous rocks, high hills, and variegated wide-spread woods adorn the winding banks of the Irthing; a river remarkable for its rapid course over a rude, rough, rock-shapen, sometimes tumbling down considerable heights when its hollow murmurs delight the ear long after the eye loses sight of it..

"Were I just rich enough to lay my leg across my hobby-horse, I would visit Gilsland again and again; and why not sit in some sequestered bower, piping the hours away happily with some good natured dulcimer, and

Ladies and gentlemen taking the waters at Gilsland Spa in 1838

mingle soft kisses according to the dictates of virtue, while the wild birds around were chaunting their love songs, and all nature inspiring the soul with harmony?" Poor Robert! Despite nature's beauty he still returns to his obsession with the ladies! Sadly he has no lady friend with him in this otherwise sylvan glade!

He went on: "But alas, I am wandering! This is one of the many pastoral delights I can only enjoy in idea; none of nature's fairest works accompany me in my rambles, for unluckily I am in want of that secret yellow charm which has tempted the sexes from the days of Grandmother Eve, yea, even to the present day!"

Contrary Robert! Elsewhere in his diary he wrote: "I am always pleased and can truly say the happiest part of my life is spent in the midst of those sublime and picturesque scenes, where Nature, robed in all her wild grandeur, seems to say `Behold me, 0 man, in my most captivating attire'."

"On arriving at the well, the qualities of whose waters I am ignorant of, except that according to vulgar opinion they heal and cure everything, and nourish those seeds of love which, taking root, bend often to Gretna Green, we beheld many sickly looking brethren and sisters who all seemed anxious to escape from the terrific leveller. Some were greedily swallowing copious draughts, as if every tumbler of water invigorated the system, others were feebly climbing the high hill with a supply in bottles, as I conjectured, for those who were so weak, or had crawled so far down the hill of life that they were unable to creep to the grey rock and quaff it in its purity; such a sight diffused a gloom over my mind, though I had determined on leaving Carlisle that this day should be spent in pleasurable contemplation. My spirits were considerably above par, all to which my companion never ventures from a port without a cargo of cheerfulness, and that, bye the bye, is worth ninety-nine times the stock of gravity.

Sterne, my favourite Sterne, has somewhere said I never could - and I never can - nay, I never will, believe that we were sent into this world to go sorrowing through it'." The Reverend Laurence Sterne was the author of Tristram Shandy, a book popular with Robert. He had also published two volumes of Parson Yorick's tongue-in-cheek sermons. Now, perched on the hillside, Robert considered the vicissitudes of life: "Gladly would I subscribe to Yorick's Shandean philosophy; but when we consider the buffeting, the back-bitings, and never-ceasing attacks on the venomous parts of mankind, to which may fairly be added a thousand hair©breadth escapes we have to accomplish against the relentless tyrant, who commonly calls when we are least prepared to give him welcome - 1 say when this is considered need it be wondered at that poor half-hunted mortals now and then sit down by the wayside and pour forth a sad complaint to a pitiless world. Not that man shall create to himself beings to keep his mind continually off the rack of discontent - the thought is worse than madness; for lunacy knows intervals of real happenings.

Robert called a halt to his musings to return to the scene at the Spa, claiming: "There are so many various groups assembled from all the four quarters that I know of few places where a disciple of Lavatoria can, with more convenience, put his Physionomonical knowledge in practice than at Gilsland Spaw; particularly if he be classed among us poor pedestrians who can only know Bath, Brighton, etc., by name.

"Pride here shews you his thousand antics for nothing, and displays all his kickshaws to the pallid children of disease; while ignorance puts on for this day the haughty strut of consequence; yet, generally speaking, the utmost freedom prevails; and being strangers to each other, from the ballroom down to the smoky cottage where the needy seek their comfortless penny shelter, all are treated according to appearance and behaviour."

It comes as no surprise to find Robert's eye then lighting on the pretty young girl serving behind the bar and, once again, waxing lyrical over the fairer sex! "Even the servants attend with such an air of good nature that the traveller deserves not a shilling in his purse who could hesitate for a moment to give half of it for the humble, modest curtsy and sweet smiling, sincere, 'Thank ye, sir' of beautiful little Primrose, the fair bar-maid; her personal charms are rarely to be equalled in the proud assemblies, where she (like her poor panegyrist) is not suffered to point her toe.

"Her face is pretty, and seems blooming proof of the efficacy of the waters, if any such proof were wanting! 'Tis one of those that in any corner of the earth could not fail to command admiration; and God grant this blooming bird of innocence and simplicity may never be cropped by the rude destroyers of virtue, for such everywhere abound, to the utter disgrace of many; we seldom behold the combination of charms that are seen in this Nymph of the Rock." From the contemplation of Primrose's beauty Anderson returns to that of nature and the Spa's attractions: " Neither pains nor expenses have been spared to render the few walks around the fountain of health at once easy and pleasant, which, in Mr C bespeaks taste as well as consideration of his own interest; here shades are erected, and seats placed at the different windings for the convenience of many a poor debilitated son or daughter of anguish; and on these the unlettered bumpkin proudly scrawls a misspelt puzzle, a love-sick line, or his name, which is indeed the only probable way of its being read by posterity.

"Happy would it have been for thee, poor old England, had the names of the present rulers been known, but in this simple and inoffensive manner then would Plenty have smiled over thy plains, and Peace gladdened every bosom; but, alas, the cries of the widows and fatherless resound from shore to shore, while famine gnaws the vital of the useful mechanic, and destruction threatens daily his once happy land - but adieu to digressions...

"Having wandered round the spring we ascended the high hill and drank each a glass of brandy by way of a preventative against cold; and again repaired to the fountain where we quaffed copiously of the salubrious waters; perhaps more than Prudence (by far the ablest physician) would have prescribed.

"We next crossed the Irthing, which here divides the counties of Cumberland and Northumberland, and winding up a romantic steep height, made easier, however, by seats being placed for the wearied or infirm, we took a peep at Wardrew, a small, but neat, well-built mansion, the residence of ? Pickering, Esq.,. Here the prospect is delightful while the eye is confined to the neighbouring banks of the of the river which winds its course in the deep valley, but the country viewed extensively is chiefly a mountainous, barren waste, and, abounding with moor game, afforded great pleasure to such as are steeled against humanity and delight in the sound of the slaughtering gun..."

"Here the contemplative traveller may sit and at a distance below examine the variety of character who resort to this healing spring; nobility and gentry for pleasure; fortune hunters and rakes to decoy or ruin the innocent; dashing sprigs of shopmen to shew their silk stockings; and many, too many, wretched creatures who only trail on an existence, come here to prevent disorders, or combat them, which already seem to be hurrying them to the grave. "From Wardrew and its winding walks my curious companion led me to see old Bett, the waterwoman who has long been well-known here; but is ever ready to serve first the well-dressed stranger and poor Bell not unfrequently receives a silver present from their leaving Gilsland. Her humble hovel is remarkably clean, but had much of a hospital in its inward appearance, serving as a receptacle for those who move in the lower walks of society, and find little pleasure at any time in this world, but particularly in quest of the coy maid Health.

"Her face would please Fuselli, or any of our Royal Academicians; particularly when studying the witches in Shakespeare's MacBeth. Time has, after sixty or seventy winters, given it the appearance of a piece of old brown parchment covering a heap of bones; she is nevertheless extremely active, and in her broad, disgusting dialect trolls many a rough-spun story with some humour; at the same time there is so much simple, honest civility in her manners that strangers may spend an hour in a worse way than by smoking a pipe over auld Betsy's ingle. Happy old creature! Thousands who look down with contempt on that withered shadow of an arm, which is stretch'd out towards them with a tumbler of water, have reason to envy thee; since virtue and vice have each a due reward or punishment."

Robert was in solemn mood as he wrote: "Health! May thy clear waters flow an endless blessing, healing the afflicted so that the virtuous may live to do good, and the vicious turn to their duty; I bid thee farewell; and think of my youth when the blush of health bloomed on my cheek, but these joyous hours are fled, never, never to return. A pale wanderer, I am doomed to tread the dark vale of life, amidst briars and thorns, without a friend to share my load of sorrow. Hope no more can fill my bosom with rapture; and content, on whose silken lap I was wont to repose, has long , long fled from my silent dwelling."

As ever, he moved quickly from philosophical musings to tales of the countryside. From treading the dark vale of life he was back tramping Cumberland! Gilsland produced tales of murder, theft, forgery and clodhopper gluttony!

"My companion and I were looking at a small white clump of rocks, which, at the distance, of two or three hundred yards, wore the appearance of an old woman washing; when hunger, that plague to the poor man, began to cause an uneasy craving within us; and led by ravenous smells, the rattling of plates, and many preparations for a kind of general engagement we drew near the scene of action and had the good fortune to get a seat at a small table in the corner of the hall where we could snugly quiz about thirty mouths all moving with wonderful dexterity. Our attention was confined to a lusty, raw, ill-looking Northumbrian clodhopper, who dined at the same table, and with his lanky, flaming-headed pasteboard looking son, about seventeen, seemed as they had travelled a long journey for the express purpose of swallowing four pounds weight each at the small expense of one shilling. "0 that some Fielding of the present day had but seen this square-mouthed monster, who, regardless of plate, slashed slices from a leg of lamb, these, great or small, were quickly conveyed to an extended mouth like an oven, which, becoming too full, he strained and chewed with such pain that his impudent looking eyes seemed at times bursting from their sockets; nor had the booby sense to refrain from talking, though the sounds of his voice, which was of the most dissonant tone, only expressed a wish for more, like an angry child when it loses the breast, or insinuated that we were fools for not brutifying ourselves, it being all of a price. His son Davey was an excellent, tho' quiet, copyist, of a parent so civilised; and played his part with a voracious dexterity seldom equalled by a two-legged animal : yea in such a manner as will be never forgotten by two present.

We ought, in common justice to an obliging landlord to have dropped a hint to prepare proper food for those speaking brutes who are unfit for society, and have cautioned him against sending Cheshire cheese to table by far that day, on account of the weight they had eaten."

"About a mile from Gilsland stands Mumps Hall; a name well known to every Cumbrian. Here, a century ago, lived the notorious Meg; who, according to tradition, caused several hawkers and travelers to be murdered in her house; for the purpose of obtaining the cash they carried. Turnpike roads were then unknown; nor were country banks, which indeed secure public property, yet become a public curse. A story which has, I believe, truth for its foundation, is told of a wine cooper who fell, a sacrifice to this she-devil, or some of her infernal gang; several of whom were apprehended and tried at Carlisle, but for want of sufficient evidence the whole were acquitted. "Meg lived to a great age, the terror of the neighbourhood; where many of her descendants may yet be found under the name of Carrick.

"The Hall, as it is called, is a mean looking brick building g, now a public house; and the present tenant being unwilling it should lose its notoriety has for some time let lodgings to vagrants of every description; for a few months ago a gang were apprehended here and are under confinement at Carlisle, who had long carried on the infamous traffic of vending forged notes.

"Having drawn a pint here we trudged on through many small villages, leaving Naworth Castle on the right; and after an hour's rest at Brampton, proceeded to Carlisle, where we arrived at 11 o'clock, quite fatigued, of course, having walked upwards of thirty miles on the hottest day I remember."

Away from the countryside there were also city delights. George Crowther, who edited a 1907 edition of the Cumberland Ballads, told of Robert's nights out with a workmate in one of the city's inns:

"A weaver, named Jack Lust, was a boon companion of Anderson during his latter days. Jack was a good singer and sang several of the Cumberland Ballads in capital style. The two comrades used to meet together at the French Horn public House, opposite the gaol, kept by Joe Purdie, a nephew of the Bard.

"Anderson would say `Come, Lusk, sing us Soldier Yeddy again, or Reed Robin, or the impatient Lassie."

Robert loved to tell the tale behind the writing of `Reed Robin'. "This song was occasioned by a redbreast visiting for five years my retired apartments in the centre of Carlisle. He commonly gave me his first cheerful strain in the beginning of September; and sang his farewell to the noise and smoke of the town in April. So tame was the merry minstrel that he frequently made a hearty repast within a few inches of the paper on which I wrote."

Despite his delight in the countryside and the city carousing in later years Robert became a morose and bitter man who had to struggle to exist. He moved to Hayton in 1823, recording the move in his `farewell to Carel' and many of his later poems were written there.

Again the Reverend Ellwood: "The poet at times seems o have sunk into those fits of deep depression to which poets in all ages, and under all conditions, seem to have been subject, and he appears at times to have held that same morbid fear of the workhouse that Burns, in his latter years, had of the jail. There was much to depress him. No-one can realise this fully who has not read through and collated his manuscripts, and seen the most careful way in which he has written and rewritten and worked out his subjects, some of them with most careful analysis. They take in a range of subjects from what were evidently intended to be Epic poems and Plays down to those terse popular songs and ballads which will live while the Cumbrian dialect lives, and posses a talismanic influence while Cumbrian can grasp the hand of Cumbrian in the strong assurance that `Canny ol' Cumberland caps them aw still.'

Age and want, an ill-matched pair, were rapidly stealing upon him, his profession was fast becoming a decaying industry in which he could not get work if he would. In one of his hitherto unpublished poems seems to refer to such a state of depression when he says:

How many aye are wrapt in care,

Whea ne'er a mortal wad oppress,
Wheyle others plenty daily share,
Still wishin brothers in distress.
Years fifty-five now owre are flown,
Sin furst on this weyl warl aw gaz'd;
Weel rear'd by twea in want aye thrown,
And leyke them aw mun ne'er be raised.

The sad little poem was written in 1825, when he had only eight more years to live.

The Reverend Ellwood described the last years of his life:

"He was very far from comfortable in his circumstances in the latter years of his life, having fallen into the vice of intemperance which, it need not be observed, robs men of their purses as well as their senses, and in poor Anderson's case made him 'poor indeed.'

"True, it may be urged in palliation of his dissipations that he was a great favourite among his fellow Citizens, and his company was much courted at the convivial board. At any rate it is known that for some years before his death he became sadly changed. His mind became soured and distempered, and his person presented a hapless picture of indigence and misery. As Ben Johnson observes he was one of the 'poor starved poets boasting of nothing but a lean visage peering out of a seam-rent suit.'

"The fear that he would end his days in the workhouse haunted his imagination to an extent almost to induce the belief that he was a Monomaniac in this respect.

"The writer of these few remarks has frequently heard him express his dread that such would be his fate. However such a misfortune was spared him. A few of his best friends entered into a subscription to provide for him in the latter days of his life, and much to their honor, he was comfortably lodged in Annetwell Street, in his native City, where he expired on Thursday evening, the 26th of September, 1833, from the general breaking up of his constitution. On the morning of the following Sunday his remains were respectfully interred in St Mary's churchyard, which is in his native parish. A large number of his fellow citizens, who entertained towards him the warmest feelings of attachment as a Friend and admiration as a poet, followed in procession."

Tributes to Robert Anderson's genius have long been paid over the years: Bishop Mandell Creighton, in his book "Carlisle", said: "Anderson was not a great poet because he had not a lofty soul; but he is intensely Cumbrian and draws a vivid picture of the actual life of the Cumbrian peasantry. "Their drinking bouts, their uncouth gallantry, their rural festivities, the humours and adventures of Carlisle Fair, and suchlike scenes are set forth with a keen relish and with the force of truth. The pathos, the nobility, and the aspirations of the higher nature scarcely ever come within Anderson's view; his limits are narrow, but within his limits his hands are firm."

James Walker, in the Carlisle Examiner of October 10, 1865, in an article on songs and ballad of Cumberland, wrote: "Anderson's popularity in his native county is much greater than any of his compeers, and he owes it chiefly to the unrivalled skill and force with which he has delineated their manners and customs of the Cumbrian peasantry of his time - manners and customs most of which have passed away before the march of progress. Considered simply as a poet - not as a word-painter of the social phases of human existence as they came under his notice in the contracted sphere in which he moved - he is decidedly inferior to most of his brother bards. But it is not the part of the critic to set up a high standard of excellence and then condemn the writer whose works fall short of it. Justice requires that an author be judged solely by by the measure of his powers; and, applying this test to Anderson, it must be said that, on the whole, he has done the work he chiefly set himself to do well, far better, probably, than any other could have done it "The greater part of his poems indubitably prove that he was gifted with a special talent, describing with force of language and fidelity to nature the outward phases of human life © which poets of the highest genius seldom possess, and thus his songs and other lyrics, racy as they are of the soil which inspired them, have an enduring value, and can never fail to instruct and entertain rich and poor alike.

"Though Anderson was a clever humourist, and has written many poems which irresistibly provoke us to laughter, he seldom shines as a satirist; but he sometimes does send a winged shaft straight to its mark with crushing force. For instance, in `Feckless Wully' he has happily hit off a failing too often met with in the world."

In 1853 'Hamilton's British Minstrel' said of him: "There are few people in England, who, during the last forty years, have not been gratified at fireside parties, or at clubs, with some of this author's songs; and in the North of England there are none of any class who are strangers to their graphic familiarities. The Cumberland Ballads are sung by the rural population in the house and in the field, in solitude and in society; and both tears and toil have been dispelled or softened by their influence." Yet few people out of the town of Carlisle know anything of the author's life, though the native region of his songs comprehends broad and populous districts, and although their popularity reaches far beyond that region, Anderson's ballads can never become universally popular because of his inveterate adherence to local dialect and local imagery. But that circumstance renders them the more popular when the dialect and the imagery are felt to be pleasantly familiar. There are in most of his pieces sentiments which touch the chords of human nature; and which, if disentangled from a profuse display of Cumbrian peculiarities, would find for his muse a name and place in every circle of society.

"Though not yet claiming a high place in poetic literature, his ballads are well worth public attention. We have sailors and soldiers - as fine fellows as the united services can boast - from Cumberland and the adjoining counties; and those songs which embody their recollections of home and early days, which make them lovers of their country and their country's customs, which cheer their hearts in foreign lands and under hard fatigues - those songs must have a national value; and the biography of their author cannot be uninteresting."

Local historian William T McIntyre, in a booklet published in 1933 to mark the centenary of Anderson's death, paid glowing tribute to the Cumberland Bard, saying: " But it is in the depiction of village festivities - festivities which, in his later years were only too congenial to Anderson's taste - that the poet excels. 'Worton' and 'Codbeck' weddings, 'Cursmas Eve' celebrations at the ` Nag's Heed', `Bridewains' or `Infairs', `Upshots' or `Murry Neets' - at all of these the poet might be seen, and at all of them he was a sympathetic observer if not a partaker. The spontaneous racy humour of the Bleckell Murry Neet stands out among these descriptions of riotous junketings.

Aa lad! See a murry neet we've hed at Bleckell,
The soun' of the fiddle yet rings in mey ear;
Aw reet clipt and heel'd were the lads and the lasses,
And monie a cliver lish huzzy was theer;
The bettermer swort sat in the parlour,
I' the pantry the sweetheart cuttered sae soft;
The dancers they kick'd up a stour I' the kitchin,
At lanter the caird-lakers sat I' the loft.

"One feels, even today, as one reads this and the stanzas that follow, that the song was tossed off in the inspiration of the moment, amid the noise and bustle and odours of the gathering itself.

The very sounds of the names of the villages are music in his ears, and constantly recur in his verse:

We've Harraby, we've Tarraby,
And Wigganby beseyde
We've Oughterby, and Souterby,
An 'bys' beath far and wide.

But the steady flame of his love for his native county bursts forth in a blaze in that most often sung of all his songs - "Canny aul Cummerlan," a ballad with many variant readings in different editions of his works:

Yer buik-larnd wise gentry, that's seen monie a county,
May wreyte, preach, palaver, an brag as they will,
O' mountains, lakes, vales, rocks, woods, waters, rich meddows,
But canny aul Cummerlan caps them aw still.

McIntyre continued: "Alas for Robert Anderson, he was one of those upon whom heaven, in bestowing the poetic gift, imposed the necessity of lavishing it, and himself, upon others. Like Burns he was one of those who died from having lived too much in their large hours.

"Habits of intemperance contracted in Ireland ruined his later life. His ineradicable kindness and generosity impelled him to spend upon others the fruit of his labours. He degenerated into a querulous invalid, ever haunted by the fear of workhouse, guilty occasionally of outbursts of misanthropy/ "If ye happ'nd to say tit, him," stated one of his contemporaries, 'It's a fine morning, Mr Anderson', ten to yan bit his reply wad be 'Dust 'e tak me for a fool or a bworn idiot? I kent that lang afooar I saw thee!'

The Reverend Ellwood, writing of Robert and other Cumbrian poets, had said; "These are our poets, and these are their subjects. They serve to give us a bond of brotherhood one to another, and to bind us with still stronger ties to our hills and valleys, to our native customs and dialects, and to the remembrances of friends and he scenery amid which our lives are cast; and they seem to say to us, in the words of our own author Anderson with which I may well conclude this notice:

We help yen anudder - we welcome the stranger,
Ourselves and our country we'll iver defend;
We pay bits o' taxes as well as we're yebble,
And pray, leyke true Britons, the war had an end.
Then Cummerlan' lads, and ye lish rwosy lasses,
If some think them clownish, ye needn't feel shem;
Be merry and wise, enjoy innocent pleasures,
And still seek for peace and contentment at yem.

McIntyre said; "In an epistle to Crito, a name by which in poems he would address his friend Thomas Sanderson, the hermit philosopher of Kirklinton, who was one of the first to recognise his genius and with whom he often held sweet converse by 'the banks o' the Leyne', Anderson speaks hopelessly of his former ambitions, and regrets that he will never accomplish the work."

He had not failed! Robert Anderson had often referred to himself as a humble rhymester. What he was never to know was that, in 1906, when world-famous composer Vaughan Williams visited Carlisle he took away wit him SIX of Robert's songs!

If the old Cumberland Bard - doubtless now casting a cynical eye at the heavenly host, an ear cocked for a false note from their harps - will forgive the paraphrasing of one of his better-known lines:

The Canny auld Cumbrian caps them aw still!

JOHN HEYSHAM

The Doctor from Carlisle

The horseman urged his mount to greater efforts, speeding along English Street, lined with gable-fronted houses, the doorways adorned with Gothic arches, the doors themselves formed from thick slabs of oak clumsily attached to oaken cross bars, with, over the surface, a scattering of metal knobs that projected in imitation of the rivets and studs of mediaeval times.

The rider halted at the Town Hall, mounted the red sandstone steps, and, finding the Mayor, told him of the proclamation of peace with Napoleon Bonaparte.

It was 1814, and it was no ordinary messenger that had lathered his horse from the south to be first with the momentous news. He was John Heysham, a sixty-one year old doctor who, though born in Lancashire, adopted Carlisle, becoming one of its more famous sons as well as one of the leaders of the social circle in the Losh family moved.

Dr Heysham's arrival was no surprise for the Mayor. Said historian Dr Lonsdale: "His patriotic feeling was keen, and oft assumed a highly demonstrative form, especially during the war with France.

"When news of import were expected, no one manifested more eagerness to know of the tide of affairs than Heysham, whose impatience led him to mount his pony, and to ride three or four miles on the south road to meet the London mail, which he stopped; and on getting his information returned at full gallop to the city.Brimful of news, he sought the Mayor's house and thundered most lustily with the knocker, so as to make His Worship alive to the situation of the hour.

One of his gallops up Botchergate was ominously looked upon as a hasty retreat to the city and drew crowds of citizens after him, curious to know if Bonaparte had crossed Barrock Fell and if Carlisle was to surrender

154

without a blow!"

Heysham was a very emotional man, often deeply affected by the death toll of disasters and the battlefields. A year after the proclamation of the so-called peace he was dining with his friends, the Mounseys of Castletown, near Rockliffe, when the news of Waterloo arrived. Said Lonsdale: "He read aloud the whole story of the victory to the assembled guests, and as he read he cried and sobbed throughout."

Dr Heysham had obtained his medical degree in Edinburgh in June, 1777, but long before that had decided to make his home in Carlisle. He had first seen the city in 1774 whilst riding north to university. The journey on horseback from Lancaster to Edinburgh was one of 170 miles, an arduous trip but one that gave the traveler time and opportunity to admire and appreciate the countryside.

Heysham had taken the Roman road, going first from Lancaster to Kendal, then, after an overnight stay, went on to Penrith and Carlisle. As he followed the Eden valley he reached first Barrock Fell and then Carleton, where, spread before him was view which had Corby Woods on his right and, on the left, the lush estate of Woodside. Lonsdale continued: "On reaching Harraby Hill, and eminence but one mile distant, he obtained the best view of the city, its surrounding walls, the towering citadel, the donjon Keep of its castle, and the stately cathedral. Situated at the confluence of three rivers, and surrounded by a plain of richly green meadows, traversed by the smaller streams of he Cauda and the Peterill, the broader vale of Eden being bounded by gradually rising uplands terminating in the Scottish hills and East Cumberland Fells, Carlisle charmed Heysham at first sight, and that charm continued through life.

"He knew nothing of its inhabitants of the place and therefore had no tie to bias his judgement; it was the walled city robbed of its mediaeval and warlike frown by rich pastoral surroundings, and a landscape of awakening interest, that allured hi fancy, and eventually decided him to make Carlisle his future home."

After graduating it was only a year before, in 1778, Dr Heysham returned to live the rest of his life in St Cuthbert's Lane and eventually become the city's senior medical practitioner, urging the practice of vaccination to stamp out the killer disease smallpox. He practised what he

155

preached. In 1800 he set an example by vaccinating his youngest daughter, Isabella, when she was just one month old.

He founded the city's Dispensary, in Chapel Street, and helped Robert Mounsey establish a fever house for the city, and, in many ways, was active in improving Carlisle, especially the paving and the lighting of the streets.

He became a magistrate and was deputy-lieutenant for Cumberland and Westmorland. The busy doctor was also a shrewd businessman. In 1800 he established a cotton mill and he was also a director of an iron foundry.

His name will forever be remembered by the world of insurance. He meticulously recorded deaths in the city, noting ages, sex, home conditions, marital status, weather conditions, the influence of war or peace, the availability of food and even the seasons of the year. With this data he produced a set of "mortality tables" which were so accurate that Sun Life and the other great insurance companies of both Great Britain and the United States used them to determine life expectancy and establish the premiums they would require.

Obviously the doctor was a busy man. But he still found time to indulge in a full and active social life. Said Lonsdale: "Heysham ranked with the intellectual folk, and these formed but a small party in the Carlisle district. He was a frequent guest at the Deanery and Prebendary houses within the precincts of the Abbey when these institutions were presided over by men of notable excellence, like Dean Percy and Archdeacon Paley. Nor was he less esteemed by the first Sir James Graham, Bart., of Netherby, and his more noted son the Statesman of Victoria's reign, the excellent Henry Howard of Corby Castle, the Loshes of Woodside and other county families. The doctor liked a good dinner and its grateful accompaniments of good wine, and both were served most liberally to the visitors of Corby and Woodside." But Dr Heysham also created a smaller, more selective circle. Said Lonsdale: "He got the credit of being facile princeps, if not the founder, of a very jovial party, consisting of about a dozen gentlemen, who dined at each others houses during the winter months; for the laudable purpose, it is presumed, of lessening the dispiriting influence of fogs and gloom and of driving all care away."

There can be no doubt that when this select diners' club did meet at table all dull care was driven away. They would sit down to dinner at three o'clock and wine and dine until ten o'clock. Over the seven hours they would each drink three bottles of strong port. Said an impressed Lonsdale: "On rare occasions, such as a victory by Nelson or the dashing Cochrane, the fourth bottle to each man was held to be the right mode of rendering the fact historical! Whether three or four bottles were the order of the day, Dr Heysham went off home to there sup off his favourite nuts and to give the last strong fillip to his stomach by a hearty draught of good strong punch."

Thomas Mounsey was a member of the dozen or so who dined so well. He described some of the other three-bottle men to Lonsdale: "The Reverend Samuel Bateman, of Newbiggin Hall, originally Rector of Hardingstone in Northamptonshire, but who, on his marriage with the co-heiress of the Aglionby family, forsook Mother Church and became a country squire. Thomas Benson, a Carlisle gentleman (A steady Whig whose father had been confidential agent of the Duke of Portland) held to be reserved, if not sedate, in general society, but who, being placed under the influence of the normal three bottles, found his facial muscles relaxed and his tongue pretty garrulous.

William Dacre of Kirklinton, better known as Squire Dacre, or Billy Dacre, was a jolly old cock at all times and at all seasons of life. Springing from the loins, direct or indirect, of the great Dacres of the North, but caring more for strong drink than noble lineage, he got the credit for being the first at a feast and the last at a fray. He attended all funerals and pretty generously got drunk at them. On one occasion the mourning neighbours, under Squire Dacre's example, got so oblivious that they reached the place of interment without the coffin!

The shenanigans did John Heysham no harm. He lived until he was eighty. He died on Sunday, March 23, 1834, and was buried in the churchyard of St Mary's, Carlisle.

JOSIAH RELPH

The Poet and Schoolmaster from Sebergham

The evening sky was darkening over Warnell Fell, looming high behind the young man at the table and seat that were cut out of the natural rock that formed Cragg Top.

He gazed over the valley below, letting his eye follow the River Caldew that ribboned its way around Churchtown, the Cumberland village where, on December 3, 1712 he was born, and just a short distance from Sebergham. It was there, on Cragg Top, that he composed poetry and songs in the solitude that he preferred, for he shunned company, often by himself walking by moonlight along the river banks and through the woods, dells and valleys. It was also there that he sought the inspiration for his writing, and, in particular, where he seemed to have reflected on the hopelessness of a love for Sally Holmes, a young lady of the neighbouring valley. It was for her that he wrote a song in Cumbrian dialect:

O what a deal of beauties rare,
Leeve down in Caldew's valley!
Yet theer not yen that can compare
Wi bonny smurking Sally

O'fortune's great my Ded oft tells,
But I cry shally-wally;
I mind fortunes nor ought else,
My heart's sae set on Sally.

Let others round the table sit
At Fairs, and drink and rally;
While in a corner snug I git,
And kiss and hark wi' Sally.

*Some lads court fearful hard, yet still
Put off and drive and dally;
The Priest neest Sunday, if she will;
May publish me and Sally.*

*O how my heart wad lowp for joy,
To lead her up the ally;
And with what courage cou'd I cry
I (Josiah) tak thee Sally.*

*And sud we not a bargain strike?
I's seer our tempers tally;
For duce a thing can Josiah like
But just what likes his Sally.*

*I's feek and wait not what to de;
The Doctor and his galley
Pots will not signify a flea;
O send off hand for Sally.*

It was 1739; the young poet was the Reverend Josiah Relph.

Was he head over heels in love with Sally Holmes, or was it just a literary exercise - yet another of his poems of love?

When, in 1798, a book of his songs and poems was published, the foreword read: "Yet perhaps no poet with as many amorous effusions felt love as little as Relph. His lyre was so fond of the loves of swains and rural dames that, whenever he wished to change its notes it became, like Anacreon's, rebellious to the touch. It vibrated with the notes of love."

Until 1689 Sebergham Parish had no regular resident minister. It was that year that the Reverend James Kenyers arrived from Annan, a refugee following the abolition of the Episcopolean church in Scotland. He was to remain there for 43 years, dying in 1733.

His successor was to be Josiah Relph. William Hutchinson's History of Cumberland said of him: "His parentage was low, but not mean." Josiah was one of three sons and a daughter. His father John was a "statesman", owner of a small landed estate inherited in turn from his father and worth about £30 a year.

His early education was at Appleby, under a Mr Yates. Hutchinson said of this schoolmaster: "Few men have had the reputation of sending out into the world so many good scholars. At fifteen Relph went to the university at Glasgow, where, we are told, he gave some distinguished proofs of a remarkable genius."

Sadly a lack of money ended his time in Glasgow. He returned to Sebergham where he first taught at a small grammar school before taking Holy Orders and being appointed to the perpetual curacy of Sebergham. It brought him thirty shillings a year. It was not a fortune, but it was sufficient. His income, said Josiah: "Was too great for contempt, and for envy too small."

At that time Sebergham, it would seem, urgently needed a crusading minister! According to Hutchinson those who lived in the village were unpolished, rude and ignorant. They believed in witches, ghosts and apparitions. "They considered the Sabbath as grateful, as only for the relaxation it afforded them from their labours; as a day of recreation rather than a day devoted to religious exercises; it was generally spent in tumultuous meetings in ale-houses or in the rude diversions of football."

The Reverend Kenyers had tried to reform them but had no luck.

Describing Kenyers, Hutchinson gave clear clues as to why he failed: "He was an austere man and his religion gloomy and unsocial, his conversation distant and reserved and his manners ungracious. Attacking and roundly condemning all amusements, even the most innocent, he lost by his moroseness what else he might have gained by the blameless tenor of his life. His parishioners pitied, despised and neglected their pastor while he gave them up as desperately abandoned, profligate and irreclaimable." Josiah's style was in complete contrast. He encouraged his flock to become more sophisticated. Hutchinson said: "To him in great measure must be attributed that elegance of conversation, esteem for learning and reverence for religion which travellers, even of the present day, observe in a people whose ancestors were tutored by Mr Relph."

Josiah had not had a happy boyhood. His diary revealed some dark days of his youth. Said Hutchinson, who had access to some of the pages: "He had a step-mother who seems to have been harsh and unkind to him and a beloved sister, all of which he submitted to and bore with pious resignation. With her, as perhaps was natural, the father seems to have sided against the son; an injury which he felt more poignantly from his having 'either entirely, or very near, made up to him all the expense he had been at in his education.' From his pupils too, and their parents, he seems sometimes to have met with unkind returns."

Josiah's tall, thin figure would stand at the school doors and wonder whether it was all worth the effort. His diary for January 21, 1737, read: "When any of the boys under my care do not make such improvement in learning and goodness as, from my endeavours, I might be justified in expecting; and also, when they leave the school without expressing that gratitude which I think I might have looked for, or when the parents disapprove of my methods or discipline, let me be particularly on my guard not to abate of my care of those still left in my charge, and regarding the censures I am exposed too, so far as only as that I may amend what, on a partial self examination, I find to be really wrong, let it be my consolation to recollect, that, if I do my duty in the station of life to which the good providence of God has called me, though I miss my reward here I shall not finally go unrewarded." It was his long-winded way of philosophically saying: "I'll get my thanks in heaven!"

It must have been a daily battle. Although his constitution was not strong he had a strict personal regime, his meals consisting of vegetables and milk, his only drink was water. His lifestyle was summed up by a contemporary who said that the whole year with him was one meagre Lent. Even at Christmas, when every Cumbrian villager was making merry, "he remained a solitary instance of sobriety and a guarded temperance."

The simplicity of this way of life may have contributed to his ill-health. The black shadow of the dread disease consumption hung over him, and, despite his friends begging him to rest from his school-teaching he carried on. Ignoring their advice was to lead to his early death.

Josiah knew well that his was not to be a long life. He was quite philosophical about it - one of his private prayers, written at the table in the rock, went: "Give me grace, O God, always to have charity for the bad, and civility to all; whilst yet I resolve to have intimacies but with few. May I hate nothing but vice, and love nothing but virtue. And whilst I continue, as I

161

ought, to consider the glory of God, and the salvation of my own soul, as the main end which I propose to myself, teach me to consider present suffering as an earnest of future enjoyment; and even sickness and sorrow as sent in mercy to prepare me for that better state which cannot now be very distant." He was a solitary man, accustomed to walking alone at night. Said Hutchinson: "To his solitary contemplation and night thoughts in the churchyard, without any light, or a light only sufficient to render darkness visible, his sundry audiences were indebted for those sermons which the editor of his poems refer to as testimonies to his piety and industry. The awe, excited by the footsteps of Relph at this unusual hour, is not yet effaced from the memory of the aged villager."

As a schoolmaster Josiah was a strict disciplinarian but the pupils he sent out into the world were of the highest standard.

One distinguished ex-pupil was Thomas Denton, who later was to publish a collection of Relph's poems. He had gone up to Queen's College Oxford, taking his Master's degree in 1752, before becoming curate to Dr Graham, of Netherby Hall, at Arthuret and Kirkandrew's churches.

Hutchinson said of his school: "That he sent out of it many good scholars is well-known but how much of this is to be attributed to his strictness we leave others to determine. He himself was certainly a man of very considerable attainments in literature. This is proved not only by the general esteem of many contemporary men of learning, with whom he lived on terms of friendship, but also by those of his translations from the classics which have been published."

Hutchinson described his final hours: "A few days before his death he sent for all his pupils, one by one, into his chamber to be a witness to his dying moments. A more affecting interview it is not possible to conceive. One of his pupils, still living, acknowledges that he never thinks of it but with awe; it reminds him, he says, of the last judgement.

"The dying saint was composed, collected and serene."

He died, unmarried, on July 26, 1743, aged just thirty-two and was buried in the family plot in Sebergham Churchyard.

The village where he did so many good works was remarkably loth to remember him. More than fifty years were to pass before the Cumberland-born Rev Jonathan Boucher, who owned a small estate in the parish, initiated an appeal to pay for a monument in Sebergham Church. He also composed the epitaph.

Said Boucher: "These epitaphs were written under an expectation that the inhabitants would be happy to concur in raising a monument by subscription, as most respectful to Relph and most creditable to them. But, when it was proposed to them, it met with no encouragement." Despite the lack of enthusiasm by the locals a monument was put up; the Cumberland Pacquet of August 5, 1794, told the story: "The Reverend Mr Boucher, of Epsom, in Surrey, has, with a generosity peculiar to himself, erected a plain but elegant monument in Sebergham Church to the memory of the Reverend Josiah Relph, who first introduced a taste for true classic learning and elegant literature into that parish, which is still successfully cultivated on the banks and in the vale of Cauda." Translated from the Latin, Boucher's tribute read:

On the North Side of this Church-Yard (the particular spot being only marked by a plain Stone bearing the Initials of his Name) Are deposited all that was mortal of JOSIAH RELPH, THE POET OF THE NORTH A Learned diligent and conscientious Schoolmaster; An Exemplary Parish Priest; a good Man And The Ornament, the Delight & the Blessing of SEBERGHAM

He died on the 26th June, 1743
IN THE 32ND YEAR OF HIS AGE;
His Works can never die
I, Decus; I, Nostrum!
The epitaph ended:
By this plain Stone to shew for this our Bard
Tutor'd by him, who teaches still, though dead,
We and our Sons with Gratitude will tread
The sacred Spot, where his lov'd Ashes lie
Till Time shall cease, and his own works shall die.

A man whose days were few if you sum his years: but if you properly view his active Virtues they were long and many; for he, with the deepest regret of all but to his own solid and endless gain, left this uncertain Abode before he had completed his 32nd year on 24th June, 1743.

Here the translation was not entirely correct; Relph died on June 26th. The last few lines of this epitaph came from the pen of the Reverend

John Stubbs, assistant curate of Sebergham. They declared: "That Oblivion might not cast a Shade upon these his Virtues, the REV JONATHAN BOUCHER, induced by no Kindred Ties and totally unknown to this departed Genius, placed this Monument 1794."

Several editions of Josiah's book of poems were produced after he had died. In 1747 the first edition was printed by Robert Foulis in Glasgow for a Mr Thomlinson, a Wigton bookseller. In 1797 a second edition was printed by W. Thompson of Carlisle with a biography by Thomas Sanderson and a pastoral elegy on his death, and in 1798 a third edition, printed by J. Mitchell in Carlisle was illustrated by Bewick woodcuts depicting village scenes.

Joisiah's home was Monkhouse Hill, where once was displayed his poem "On Tea" and the beginning of "Haytime, or the Constant Lovers".

JOSEPH SIMPSON

The Society Artist from Carlisle

The man sitting for a preliminary sketch - to be used for a later portrait - was restless, his attention continually diverted by the colour and activity around him. His lady wife had to keep prodding him with her parasol, exclaiming: "George, do remember that Mr Simpson is trying to sketch you!"

It was 1936; George happened to be King George V, the lady prodding him was Queen Mary.

The outdoor, makeshift, studio? Nothing less than the Royal Box at Epsom racecourse from which the Royal couple would see Mahmoud win that year's Derby. The artist was Carlisle-born Joseph Simpson, a man thought by some to have had no formal art education, but in reality had been a pupil under Herbert Lees, head of the Carlisle School of Art. Earlier education had been under the Reverend Alexander Davidson

The school, in Finkle Street, was a successor to the Carlisle Society for the Encouragement of Fine Arts, established in 1822, leading to a new Academy of Arts in 1823, which, in 1854, became the Carlisle School of Art.

The portrait of King George, who was to die soon after it was painted, now hangs in the National Portrait Gallery, along with many other paintings by Simpson. But his works were not restricted to formal portraits; he was a versatile artist able to work in many mediums.

He was a master of caricature. Old-time journalist Jack Booth, in his biography Palmy Days, told the tale: "On the outbreak of the first world war it was decided at an editorial conference of the staff of Town Topics, of which I was a member, that a weekly cartoon of some figure in the public eye would be a valuable feature, and a few days later Edgar Wallace, who had recently joined the paper, brought Joseph Simpson down to the office in Essex Street. From the first one realised one was in the presence of a strong and unique

A self portrait by Joseph Simpson

personality." Edgar Wallace, novelist and playwright, was at the time also a journalist.

Booth paid testimony to the artist's skills, saying: "Simpson's success as illustrator, poster designer, master-etcher and painter, was due entirely to his great natural gifts, which amounted to genius."

He was well qualified as a judge of character; he had been on the staff of the Sporting Times - known familiarly as The Pink 'Un, - the turn-of-the-century publication for bon-viveurs that, as well as racing, covered the theatre and restaurants.

Frank Brangwyn by Joseph Simpson

Booth had rubbed shoulders with the cream of London's West End world, was a close friend of Sir Herbert Beerbohm Tree, the actor/manager who first owned the Haymarket Theatre and later Her Majesty's. Tree was a great character actor, playing Falstaff, Fagin, Shylock and Micawber.

Another friend was Charles Cochran, renowned for his lavish revues, annual events at the London Pavilion in the 1920s and 1930s, and featuring the 'Cochran Young Ladies'. They were pretty, and could sing and dance. One, Marjorie Robertson, later changed her name and became famous as the actress Anna Neagle. He also knew Rudyard Kipling, and in his time wrote of stars of the Edwardian stage that included Lily Langtry, Ellen Terry, Sir Henry Irving and Oscar Wilde.

For a short time the young Joseph Simpson had worked for Carlisle's Hudson Scott Company, and at the age of seventeen collaborated with the Reverend Hugh McPherson - in 1897 the vicar of Allonby and a prolific writer on natural history - on his book The History of Fowling. His illustrations for this brought him his employment in Edinburgh, creating commercial artwork, but in his spare time he did some watercolours, several of which were exhibited at the Royal Scottish Academy. A series of bookplates led to caricatures for London and American papers. Life was good for Joseph Simpson; he was a young artist, enjoying a Bohemian way of life. Other young Edinburgh artists would meet in his studio in Castle Street, forming a club for sketching, as well as for discussion and social activities. They called the club the SPO. For the uninitiated the letters meant nothing; in reality they stood for their favourite food - sausages, potatoes and onions!

A Scottish magazine, The Student, produced for the university population, told of his lifestyle in Edinburgh: "If you go down to Albany Street to call on him at any hour of the forenoon you are pretty sure to find both himself and a packet of Gold Flake to welcome you, and any amount of time to smoke and any amount of pictures to look at and to hear his views about.

"In the silence of sleep time t'is another matter. You may knock hard and burst your knuckles knocking, but in spite of the glint of lamplight under the door there will be no acknowledgement of your condescension, and you will clatter back downstairs in the dark with sore fingers and a melancholy wonder in your mind at the ways of artists."

But Simpson needed a wider field for his work and in 1905 left Edinburgh for London where he soon became famous for his striking black and white work and his gift for portraiture. Admirers of his work said that he had an uncanny knack of reproducing, in life-like outline, the features of his subjects. Praise came from all sides; playwright George Bernard Shaw claimed that a caricature of himself brought out his character better than others had managed to.

Joseph Simpson was the archetypal artist. Journalist Booth described him: "Sartorial conventions meant nothing to him. The old tweed hat must have covered his head for a generation, the too-long trousers, his too-short waistcoat that in moments of excitement or unwanted exertion revealed

James Pryde by Joseph Simpson

One of Simpson's famous silhouettes

braces and buttons, the same Richmond Gem cigarettes, the same untidy wisp of hair - Simpson was unchangeable. His outlook on life was peculiarly his own."

Booth told how Simpson would not draw just anybody - he had his own set of rules - he had to like their face!

With his friend James Pryde and sculptor Barney Seale he was in the entrance hall of the Adelphi Hotel when he met Southport architect George Tonge, later to join Simpson's circle of close friends.

Booth recalled that Simpson, peering over the rim of his spectacles, said: "I don't know you sir, but I like your face. Will you join us?"

But Booth also told of Simpson's embarrassing habit of looking at people strictly from the etchable standpoint. An acquaintance, a great admirer of his art, asked Simpson if he would do an etched portrait of him, saying he was prepared to pay one hundred guineas.

The artist replied: "My dear fellow, I would not do it if you gave me two hundred guineas!"

"Why", asked the bewildered acquaintance.

"Because I do not like your face".

Said Booth: "His objection was the entirely personal objection of the master etcher, who viewed the proposal entirely from the master-etcher's standpoint and saw his subject as an etching, pure and simple."

But Simpson was quite able to mock himself. A quick self-sketch shows him as a man with a stubbly chin and a mop of untidy black hair and his spectacles perched crazily on the end of his nose.

In 1918 he was commissioned as the official war artist for the R.A.F. and was stationed in France. His drawings of life in front of the trenches as well as behind them, earned him a C.B.E. After the war his work was exhibited in Munich, Venice, Florence and Stockholm. One in particular - The Bombed House - used to hang in Tullie House.

During his lifetime he created just over fifty original etchings. Critics agree that he created two great masterpieces, one of his close friend and fellow etcher, Frank Brangwyn, and his portrait of his inseparable friend, artist, James Pryde.

Published in London in 1924 in a signed edition of 150, James Pryde was said to be a powerful study of character and expression, and one of the finest etchings of the early twentieth century.

The quality of his work was instantly acknowledged by the art experts; the British Museum in London has almost twenty of Simpson's original etchings in its permanent collection.

He was a generous man. A kind action or a small service would be rewarded by a gift of one of his prized etchings.

Booth told a story of one who received one of his gifts who obviously was not an art-savant. "On a visit to dine with a friend at his hotel he accidentally left behind his portfolio of etchings and was unable to trace it. Some months later the friend was staying at the same hotel and Simpson once again dined with him. The receptionist remembered him. 'Oh, I think I have a parcel of yours, sir,' she exclaimed. She had, and tears of relief filled the artist's eyes as he took back his treasured prints.

'I must give that delightful girl an etching,' he said to his host. 'What do you think she would like best?' And together they selected his famous "A Grenadier of the Guards" Her reply was: "Oh thank you so much Mr Simpson. Have you just drawn this specially for me?"

He painted King Edward VII and Queen Alexandre. The London world of literature and theatre had also opened its doors to him. In 1932 Simpson created a portfolio of pictures to illustrate J B Priestley's new play, Angel Pavement. He painted Treasure Island author Robert Louis Stevenson. He drawings included famous actress Sarah Bernhardt, the actor Augustus John and Edith Sitwell, the novelist and poet who belonged to the famous Sitwell literary family.

He was meticulous in his choice of artists' materials. Said Jack Booth: "For his etchings Simpson laid great store on the importance of old, hand©made paper, and his search for this was never©ending. My last memory of him was his arrival one afternoon at the office of Town Topics with a brown paper bundle under his arm which he unwrapped on my desk and proudly displayed sheet after sheet of priceless old paper he had just unearthed from some bookseller's shop - sheets bearing the date and watermark of 1610."

Typical of the man was his instant decision never again to caricature. The blame must rest with the Daily Mirror, then part of the giant Harmsworth publishing group.

In July 1907 a business exhibition was held at Olympia. Hoardings in the streets of London displayed a striking poster by Simpson. Depicting the "ideal businessman". A grim faced tycoon glowered out over passers-by.

Jack Booth told the story: "All London stared at the arrogant, cruel-looking face, a face which bore the stamp of a living personality, one who had accumulated vast wealth. The broad, low, forehead, cold piercing eyes, heavy moustache drooping over a steely jaw, suggested immediately the face of Pierpoint Morgan. In 1891 John Pierpoint Morgan had organised the merger of Edison General Electric and Thompson-Houston Electric Company to form General Electric, which then became the country's main electrical-equipment manufacturing company. After financing the creation of the Federal Steel Company he merged it with the Carnegie Steel Company to form the United States Steel Corporation. By 1902 Morgan controlled over 5,000 miles of American railroads.

Alfred Harmsworth, owner of the Daily Mirror, was upset at the idea of the ideal businessman being an American.

His newspaper launched its attack: "The first thing that strikes a fresh arrival in London as the present time is a hideous face on all the hoardings, features contorted with greed, forehead corrugated with worry furrows, eyes bulging out as if an attempt to hypnotise the passer-by. At first you must think it designed to advertise the life of some notorious criminal, or a patent nerve tonic, or a new pill, the idea being that anyone who in the least resembles the poster needs medicine very badly indeed. These guesses are quite wrong. It is really an advertisement of the Business Exhibition at Olympia, and a very clever advertisement too, for it insists on being looked at. But it is a gross libel on the English businessman... It is a cruel face. It is a criminal face. It is the face of a man who would stick at nothing to make his business go. It is also a face which proclaims the narrow mind, heedless, in its preoccupation, of all the interest and wonder and beauty of the world..."

The newspaper thundered on, ending its piece by saying: "To suggest that this is a fair type of English businessman is ridiculous. To hold it up as a type to be followed would be a crime."

Said Booth: "All of which would seem to be extremely unflattering to Mr Pierpoint Morgan, who was not, at that time, in the Harmsworth graces."

Joseph Simpson's reply was written with a pen dipped in acid: "On reading the attack on my poster I thought that the writer must be possessed of the quintessential soul of the man in the street; but a moment's reflection brought me to the fact that the man in the street at least understands the qualities that go to make success in commerce." His reply was a lengthy one. He ended by saying: "The portrait is that of the great American financial genius who has loomed largest in the imagination of city men since Rhodes passed from us. If the writer would commission me to design a poster depicting a British Napoleon of commerce I must do it, but I have now turned my back on caricature."

Said Booth: "From that moment he abandoned the medium by which he was able to express his keen and discerning humour. He never forgave the critic who caused his decision."

Joseph Simpson, illustrator, poster designer, master etcher and painter, died on January 30, 1939, aged just 59. He left a wife, formerly Miss Lucy Sinclair Cameron, a member of a well-known Edinburgh family, and one son. Another son had died four years before him

His legacy to his home city was the set of wonderful paintings of familiar scenes and characters that appeared for many years in the annual calendars produced by city printers Charles Thurman and Sons.

Not bad for a man of whom The Student magazine once said: "You might expect milk from a millstone as facts from his past life from Mr Simpson. He leads the interviewer vaguely to believe there was no time in his existence at which he did not draw more or less. Where he learnt to draw, and by whom he was taught, are conjectures even more nebulous. The safest is that he probably taught himself".

JOHN TAYLOR & ROBERT BOWMAN

Cumbrians have made their mark in many ways. Some specialised in medicine, others took up careers in the army, in the arts, in journalism, in politics. But one man stands out from the crowd.

He was John Taylor. No gifted architect, no writer of prose and poetry, no captain of industry. Simply, this man lived to be a surprising 135 years old. More surprising, he worked for one hundred of those years. Even more surprisingly, he waited until he was sixty years old before marrying. He then went on then go on to father nine children.

John Taylor was born in 1637 at Garrigill, a village near the market town of Alston, not noted for the longevity of its inhabitants, many of whom had laboured in the lead mines of Alston Moor.

John had worked in the mines since his childhood. He started when he was just eleven years old, and was known to have been there on March 29, 1652, the day of the great solar eclipse known as "Mirk Monday".

Apart from two years spent working for the Treasury he was always a miner, first at Alston, but later moving to Blackhall, near Durham, and going from there to various mines in Scotland, including Leadhills, the silver mine near Moffat.

It was whilst he was working at Leadhills that an account of his life was sent to Dr Charles Lyttelton, the then Bishop of Carlisle, and a copy went to the Society of Antiquities. Later an 1816 edition of Magna Britannica told the tale of the old lead miner, saying: "Generally speaking the inhabitant of Cumberland who live to this protracted age are healthy, and strong, capable of performing the functions of their several stations and even partaking of the amusements of life, almost to its close."

The ghost of old John, resting outside some great mine in the sky, remembering his nine children, surely would have chuckled and said "hear, hear" to that!

So would have Robert Bowman, in 1705 born in the village of Hayton. He lived to be almost 118 years old. Thomas Sanderson told his story in his "Memoirs of a Very Old Villager", written in July, 1817, who said: "Few counties in Great Britain have produced so many instances of longevity as Cumberland, which, perhaps, may be attributed to the salubrity of its mountain air, to the constitutional vivacity of its inhabitants, as well as their temperate and regular modes of life."

When we walk in churchyards we often see tombstones in memory of persons who have died at the age of eighty or ninety years. In Castle Sowerby churchyard we find the monument of a man who reached his 109th year, and in the middle of last century a woman died in the eastern part of the county at the age of 110 who could remember the siege of Carlisle by Cromwell's forces, when a horse's head sold for half a crown, about fifteen shillings of our present money.

Robert Bowman, a husbandman, lived the last forty years of his life in Irthington. In May, 1816, he was visited by Sanderson, who wrote: "I paid a visit to his humble habitation, which, like its aged proprietor, has withstood many a wintry blast. I found him lying on a couch, near the fireplace, with the roseate glow of health upon his cheeks and serenity upon his countenance that indicated the tranquility of his heart."

I approached him with all the veneration due to an old man of 112 and was happy to find that time, though it blanched his locks and furrowed his brow, had not impaired his hearing." Two years later Robert Bowman could, at night, when all else was silent, still hear the ticking of a watch that hung in a small window some yards away.

His memory was still good. He could recall the 1715 Jacobite Uprising, when the Sheriff of Cumberland mustered a posse on Penrith Fell in an attempt to halt the rebels. Butter was then three-pence a pound and eggs a penny a dozen. Wheat and potatoes had not then made their appearance in Cumberland, meat and tea were strictly the preserve of the rich. Said Sanderson: "If the Cumbrian peasant could see, smoking on his board, an oatmeal pancake and a cowed lwod (a pudding made from oatmeal and hog's lard) he cast no longing eye at the fleshpots of the more wealthy

176

countrymen."

Robert Bowman had waited until he was fifty years old before marrying and successfully taking over a small farm which provided a comfortable income. It was a loving relationship. They had several children, and Robert was heartbroken when his wife died. He never married again.

Otherwise he was a tough old Cumbrian, Said Sanderson: "He was seldom seen muffled up, he rarely wore gloves, which he considered an effeminate covering, and boots and spatterdashes were rejected for the same reason. He made it his practice to go to bed soon and rise early, and during the summer generally took a noon-day nap on some breezy bank where he enjoyed the air in all its purity.

"In this sickly, pill-taking age, a doctor's recipe was never known, for, like many other old men who have enjoyed an uninterrupted state of good health, no argument could ever convince him of the utility of the medical profession. He looks upon the great increase of physicians and apothecaries as a melancholy testimony to the credulity of modern times."

Robert Bowman died on June 18, 1823. The Carlisle Patriot recorded: "He grew weaker as the day declined, but experienced no pain. About eight in the evening he slept silently away in the arms of death at the extraordinary age of 117 years and eight months, a fruit ripe for the gathering, a shock ready for the sickle of the great reaper whose harvest, however protracted, is, nevertheless, infallibly sure."

JAMES WALLACE

The Attorney General from Brampton

Dinner parties at the splendid Streatham Park mansion were THE place to be in late eighteenth century London. The food, served on silver plate gleaming under candlelit chandeliers, would have appealed to the most fastidious gourmet; the wine would have been of the very best vintage.

For Streatham Park was the home of Henry and Hester Thrace, and Henry was the owner of the Anchor Brewery, the largest in the world, stretching, as it did, over twelve acres.

Their dinner parties were made up of the cream of London society: It was said that Mrs Thrale had a taste for literary guests and literary guests had a taste for her good dinners. Regulars at her table included Sir Joshua Reynolds, painter and President of the Royal Academy; author Oliver Goldsmith; diarist James Boswell; Sir John Hawkins, the first biographer of Dr Johnson who also had worked on Izaak Walton's Compleat Angler; Edmund Burke, MP., political thinker and orator; Dr Thomas Percy, Editor of The Tatler, Spectator and Guardian; Fanny Burney, diarist and famous court gossiper, and actor David Garrick.

James Boswell summed up the guests as "the witty and the eminent assembled in numerous companies."

Keeping company with the elite of the day, and justly so, was Cumbrian James Wallace. He had been born in the parish of Brampton and baptized on March 12th, 1730. Despite a very ordinary early education, he had taken up the law. A branch of the Wallace family had moved from Craigie House, in Ayshire, the original seat of the family that gave birth to the notorious William Wallace, and moved to Northumberland.

In his History of Cumberland William Hutchinson said: "By the fault, or misfortune, of his ancestors a very small part of these descended to Mr

Wallace; but the want of fortune was amply compensated by his industry and talents. From a common school education, which he received at Thornton, in Yorkshire, without the aid of wealth, or the support of connection, dependent solely on his own efforts, he attained the office of Attorney General, of which important situation he died possessed at the age of fifty-three."

By taking up the law James had followed family tradition; his father Thomas, who had moved to Brampton from Asholme, in Northumberland, was an attorney. How the family fortune appeared to have been in trouble is a mystery. The talented James left all this behind to rise steadily up the legal ladder: On November 22, 1754, he had been admitted to Lincoln's Inn, a year later he was admitted to the Middle Temple. In June, 1761, he was called to the bar, and in 1769 became a K.C. One year after he became a member of parliament for the Surrey town of Horsham. In April 1770 he was gifted the seat by Henry Ingram - Viscount Irwin. The Horsham seat had just eighty voters; he represented them for life, never having to face a contested election.

James Wallace was going places. That same year he had turned down the chance of becoming a Judge of the King's Bench, taking his seat in the House of Commons and becoming a staunch supporter of Lord North; North recognised his ability and his support and in 1778 James Wallace was rewarded by his appointment as Solicitor General. Two years later he became the country's top lawyer - promoted to Attorney General

As such he helped make American history, when, in March 1782 he requested leave of the House to introduce a Bill "to enable His Majesty to conclude a truce or peace with the revolted American colonies."

In later years James Wallace, when in Cumberland, lived in splendour at Carleton Hall, a mansion about a mile southeast of Penrith which had given its name to a family who were located there soon after the Norman Conquest. In 1707 the family became extinct and the manor was sold to John Pattinson; his daughter, Elizabeth, had married Thomas Simpson, and he inherited the Hall when Pattinson died. The hall then had come into the possession of James Wallace by his marriage with Thomas Simpson's only daughter, Elizabeth, born in January, 1741. James and Elizabeth, whom he had wed on January 8, 1767, were no strangers to bequests: When Thomas Simpson died in 1768 his will carried the instruction: "All my debts to be paid, particularly £5,000, which I agreed to pay as the marriage portion of my daughter on her intermarriage with James Wallace, Esq. To my dear wife £30 and to the said James Wallace and Elizabeth his wife each £20 to buy mourning."

Later in 1768 Lancelot Simpson had died unmarried. After various bequests his will read "... all the rest of my personal estate I bequeath to my niece Elizabeth Wallace, wife of James Wallace of Carleton Hall in the county of Cumberland, and I appoint her my executrix." It was no mean bequest. Lancelot had inherited Musgrave Hall, near Penrith, from his attorney father Hugh. Five years later Elizabeth was to sell it. 1768 was a tragic one for the Simpsons. Hugh, brother of James' wife Elizabeth, also died, aged just thirty-five. After several bequests he then instructed: "The residue of my real and personal; estate I leave to my dear sister Elizabeth Wallace, wife of James Wallace, of the Inner Temple, London. I appoint the said James Wallace my sole executor.

Life was not to be a continual round of London dinner parties for James Wallace. He worked hard, and in 1773 was appearing at the Easter Term of the Cumberland Assizes, retained, for one guinea, by John Wordsworth, the lawyer brother of poet William. The case revolved round ancient rights and common land at Culgaith

In 1783 James Wallace died aged 52. A brass plate in St Andrew's Church in Penrith commemorates his life.

His early death was tragic in more than one way; his career, as it should have been, was about to be rewarded by both the Inns of Law and by his country.

Said Hutchinson: "He was at the zenith of his reputation and at the moment when the highest honours his profession could offer, or his country bestow, were almost within his grasp."

Carleton Hall is now the headquarters of the Cumbria police force.